BUILDING
TODAY'S
CHURCH

BUILDING TODAY'S CHURCH

How Pastors and Laymen Work Together

LESLIE PARROTT

BAKER BOOK HOUSE
Grand Rapids, Michigan

Reprinted 1973 by
Baker Book House Company
with the permission of Beacon Hill Press
ISBN: 0-8010-6941-6

Second printing, April 1976

PHOTOLITHOPRINTED BY CUSHING - MALLOY, INC.
ANN ARBOR, MICHIGAN, UNITED STATES OF AMERICA
1976

Foreword

Among more than a score of books written by Dr. Samuel Shoemaker is one entitled *By the Power of God*. The title sounds the keynote of an effective church ministry. The need today is for the same basic principles of divine guidance and spiritual force which were characteristic of the New Testament Church.

That is what Dr. Leslie Parrott's book is all about: how a local church can utilize its potential by planning, preparing, and programming, all the while relying on the power of the Holy Spirit.

Behind the report of every growing, evangelistic church are a dedicated pastor and committed laymen who are working together under the enabling power of the Holy Spirit.

Dr. Parrott believes that for most churches the problem is not so much one of desire as it is of direction, and therein lies the story that unfolds in this volume. There are no spectacular schemes of publicity seeking, no bizarre ideas for mushroom expansion, no shortcut innovations so frequently marked by regrettable aftermaths.

Sometimes a pastor sees "direction" as a matter of better understanding the "power structure" in the church, which can be viewed either as an adversary to be opposed or as an ally to be utilized. When treated as an adversary, either he or the "power structure" emerges as victor; and if it is the latter, he is no longer in a position of leadership. But if the pastor prevails in such a senseless contest, another "power structure" will arise immediately. Furthermore, the pattern will continue, with wasted energies expended in inner conflicts, with enthusiasm and joy siphoned away and fellowship hindered. Most tragic of all, souls will go away without redemption in Christ.

There is, praise God, another alternative. The church board and pastor can reject the opponent syndrome and get on with the business of working together in the power of the Holy Spirit.

Writing a book like this, admittedly, is ticklish business. The least touch of arrogance or superiority would immediately destroy its appeal. But Les writes with humility, never as a paragon of perfection. The author is not a traditionalist, by any means, yet he honors the time-tested methods which have characterized the truly evangelical church from its beginning: the fundamental doctrines, the altar call, the Sunday evening service, Bible-centered preaching.

The message of this book is that every activity of the church can be an event to be anticipated with expectancy. When pastors and laymen understand each other better and work together under the enabling power of the Spirit, they rise to the occasion and make the most of their challenging opportunities.

—JAMES McGRAW
Professor of Preaching and Pastoral Ministry
Nazarene Theological Seminary

Contents

THE
HOLY SPIRIT
AND
PASTORAL
LEADERSHIP

CHAPTER 1

What Happened to a Church with Twelve Members

The Apostle Paul, as the first church administrator, could have been called district superintendent, general superintendent, bishop, moderator, or executive secretary; the the title would not have mattered. His assignment, under God, was to go into the major cities of his day and to begin the development of a church by preaching in the synagogues, witnessing in the marketplaces, and visiting from house to house.

However, when Paul visited the church in Ephesus, it was already organized. But it was a small church, ingrown, dominated by a few strong people. It was not growing. The Ephesus church was static and needed to be transformed. The people needed to break out of their own self-defeating ways to begin making a perceptible impact on the great metropolitan center.

I have always thought that Paul first visited Ephesus on a Monday night—probably because he held a board meeting after the service. If Paul's after-church board meeting was like many after-church board meetings, there is little difficulty in picturing the situation. The meeting was held in a nondescript room while irritated wives and children waited in the front hallway of the church. Teen-agers sat impatiently in their chariots talking glibly with one another about what was wrong with the Roman Empire. Meanwhile, in the meeting, board members were skillfully expressing their own subjective opinions about the local church without real depth insights into the reasons for their lack of growth.

There is no record of this board meeting, but it probably went something like this:

After an opening prayer, Paul began the meeting with some words of appreciation for the privilege of being there and then asked an open-ended question: "Can you tell me how the church has been going?"

Almost immediately, one of those board members stood to his feet and said, "Mr. Superintendent, I would like to tell you about the wonderful pastor we have in our church. We do not believe there is another pastor on the entire Asia Minor District who can compare with the man God has given us. He is physically handsome, tall, dark-haired, with a set of piercing eyes that always command attention. When he preaches on Sundays, people literally sit on the edges of their seats hanging on to each word as he delivers it. In fact, his name has become synonymous with eloquence throughout the city of Ephesus. People commonly refer to the eloquence of an Apollos. And we just thank God that we have had the privilege of enjoying such a wonderful pastor as our spiritual leader."

Paul responded by saying, "I thank God for the way you feel about your pastor. I have long since learned that no church can ever do a truly effective job unless there is unity about the man whom God has given them as their spiritual leader. I rejoice in this report. But what else can you tell me?"

Another board member stood to his feet and said, "Mr.

Superintendent, I would like to tell you about the wonderful lay leadership we have in our church. We doubt if there is another church on the entire district which has as strong laymen in places of responsibility as we do right here in the city of Ephesus. For instance, there is this couple, Aquila and Priscilla, who are tentmakers. They do not make ordinary tents. They make tents for royalty. And not only do they sell to the heads of state, but people come from all the surrounding territory for many hundreds of miles in every direction to do business with these good laymen. They are not only solid financial supporters of our church themselves, but have been able to hire people out of our congregation to work for them. We just thank God that we have Aquila and Priscilla as lay leaders in our church."

Paul nodded in vigorous assent. "Thank God! I rejoice to hear you have such wonderful lay leaders in your church. I have learned from experience that no church will ever do a truly effective job in the kingdom of God unless there are strong lay leaders on whose shoulders responsibility may be laid with confidence. But what else can you tell me?"

Another one of the board members stood to his feet and said, "Mr. Superintendent, I would like to tell you what a wonderful location Ephesus is for a church like ours. We don't believe there is another church on the entire district which is as strategically located. Ephesus is one of the great cities of the world. Its population of 200,000 people makes it just the right size for us to make a real impact. We have here in our community one of the seven wonders of the world, the Temple to the goddess Diana. Our city is the key metropolis between Rome and Asia. We are on the crossroads of the world by land and sea. It is the center of banking and the hub for industry. We have vision for a great church and then the possibility of organizing a school where we may train our young people to go out in evangelistic teams throughout all this part of the world."

The Apostle Paul smiled broadly as he nodded agreement to the board member who had reported on location. "I am glad to hear you are thrilled with the location of your church. I have learned that no church will ever do a truly effective job unless there is enthusiasm about the opportunities for evangelism the surrounding area affords. But what else can you tell me?"

By this time the board members began to look at one another with question marks on their faces. No one seemed to have anything else to add to the report. Finally, one of the board members said what the rest of them were thinking, "Mr. Superintendent, I guess that is just about the story with us."

Paul nodded and scanned the room as he began to speak. "I have two additional questions to ask you. What was the membership of your church last year?"

The statistical secretary looked at the book and reported that the membership in the church the previous year consisted of 12 men. (It would do havoc to most church statistics today if only the names of the men were counted in the membership.)

Paul nodded his thanks for the report and continued by asking his second question, "Can you tell me how many members there are in the church this year?"

The statistical secretary looked at the record and reported the membership this year also consisted of exactly 12 men.

A shadow must have gone across the face of Paul as he stood to his feet and began to speak. "Now let me make a little summary of what we have said thus far. You indicate to me that you have a wonderful pastor whose name is synonymous with eloquence and whose sermons each week are anticipated with great joy by the congregation. You tell me you have strong lay leadership on whose shoulders responsibility can be laid with confidence. And you tell me that your church is strategically located in one of the great cities of the world. But you also have indicated that your church is exactly the same size now as it was a year ago. And perhaps if we went back further into the records of previous years we would find that the church has hit a plateau where statistics do not evidence any kind of spiritual or numerical growth."

Clenching his fist with an extended forefinger which he used to jab holes in the air, Paul scanned the face of each board member in the room as he asked his one final question. "Have you received the Holy Spirit since you believed?"

Stunned, the board members looked at each other and back at Paul with question marks on their faces indicating confusion over the meaning of his question. Finally, one of the board members expressed the feelings of all the others when he said, "I do not think we know very much about the Holy Spirit. Certainly, we have not had any great evidence of His presence since we first believed on Jesus Christ."

This imaginative story which has its roots in the eighteenth and nineteenth chapters of Acts builds toward a great spiritual climax as Paul begins to teach and preach to these people concerning the Holy Spirit. Finally Paul lays his hands on them, and the Holy Spirit comes upon them. "And all the men," says the Bible, "were about twelve."

At least two episodes in Acts give insight into what happened in this little church so suddenly transformed.

First, the Ephesian fellowship of Christians could no longer be ignored.

At this point in the history of the Early Church there began the greatest revival recorded in the New Testament outside the Day of Pentecost. And it all started when one dozen men were filled with the power of the Holy Spirit. One church became many churches. The impact of the gospel came with such force that Ephesus could no longer ignore it. Miraculous things happened. Even the attention of the government was turned upon the congregation of Christians who had been filled with the Holy Spirit.

Visitors to Ephesus today may walk on the Boulevard of the Silversmiths, which runs the length of the ancient business district between the temple and the city library. Without doubt, Paul studied many times in that library and witnessed often to the keepers of the little shops on the boulevard. And without doubt he stood in awe, as did thousands of travelers from all over the world, as they looked at this huge temple to Diana of the Ephesians, one of the seven wonders of the world. But the impact of the small church which became transformed was so gigantic that the entire image-making business along the Boulevard of the Silversmiths was threatened. As people began to accept Jesus Christ as Lord and Master of their lives, they no longer felt a need for the replicas of the Temple of Diana or need for the small statues of the pagan goddess.

The regional director of the CIO-SSU (the Silversmith's Union) in Ephesus was Demetrius. With all of the unions, or guilds, joining together, a united protest march was organized against Paul and the Christian Church. With great placards which denounced the Church and the gospel of Christ, hordes of men swept down the Boulevard of the Silversmiths en route to the amphitheatre, which seated 13,000 people. Here the town clerk tried to bring order out of chaos by banging his gavel on the podium. But overwhelmed with their own angry emotions, the noise of the threatened idol makers could not be contained. For two hours they ranted and raved until finally their own emotional energies were drained.

With things quieting down, the city clerk again called for order and asked for the accusations against Paul. When he learned that men were angry because a man had come who preached about a God not made with hands, it may forever be to the credit of that city clerk that he banged down his gavel and dismissed the meeting, demanding that the unions go back to their places of business to meet this new kind of competition.

Certainly no one wants to pastor a church which becomes the object of angry protests and demonstrations in a community. But it also may be said that one of the worst things that can happen to a church in any town is to be ignored. If Paul were alive and pastoring today in any major city of the United States or the world, no one could predict how he might go about making an impact on the city. But one thing is certain, he would not be ignored. People would know that both himself and his church were very much alive and proclaiming with effective vigor the transforming gospel of Jesus Christ. Perhaps the gravest sin that can be committed by any church today is to retreat into a community position which allows it to be ignored.

Second, the Christian fellowship in Ephesus became opportunists in getting outside their four walls with the gospel.

In places where people do not have faith in the living God, books of magic which outline the virtues of palm reading, stargazing, and the reading of tea leaves become popular. People in Ephesus were loaded with these books. Being converted, the people no longer needed black magic. When Paul was asked what should be done, he seized the opportunity to take the church outside the tiny house where it was meeting into the larger scope of total community attention.

He said, "Monday night is often an off night in the revival. So we will get permission from the city fathers to rope off the town square in front of the library. Tell everyone to bring his books of magic and we will pile them up for a great bonfire and hold a street meeting the city will never forget."

The people came with their books of magic by the armloads. They piled them all in a great heap which was estimated to be no less than $5,000 in value, which must have been before a few rounds of inflation. While the oil was poured on and the fire lighted, the people lifted their voices in hymns of praise to God, and proclaimed the good news which had transformed their lives. Their street meeting for the burning of the books of magic made a bigger impact on Ephesus than a thousand testimony meetings inside the church building. If Paul were pastoring in a major city of the Unites States or the world, no one can predict how he might do it, but one thing is certain, Paul would take the message of the church from inside its four walls into the places people lived and worked. Using whatever opportunities were available, Paul would not be ignored, and he would not be confined to four walls in the proclamation of the gospel.

For most small churches, the transforming power of the Holy Spirit is not so much a problem of desire as it is direction. Just what can be looked for in the church that is undergoing a transformation from static statistics to a healthy growth and development?

With a yellow pad of paper, a pencil, and the New Testament, I began reading the Acts of the Apostles and the Epistles to find out what happened in the Early Church when the Holy Spirit came on a congregation. For the first three consecutive Sunday mornings in one pastorate, and numerous times during the next seven years, I preached from this text, "Have ye received the Holy Ghost since ye believed?" The reason the text came alive for me and the congregation was a clear New Testament understanding of what we could expect to have happen in our church when the Holy Spirit was poured out upon us.

To begin with, I learned this outpouring of the Holy Spirit was not only an individual matter, but actually a united experience for the total congregation. Just as one person can be filled with the Holy Spirit, so also can a church.

And second, I learned there is not only the initial infilling of the Holy Spirit in the church, but there are many subsequent outpourings of renewal of the Spirit on the church.

Although a list of many passages and verses was made

in this initial study of the New Testament outpourings of the Holy Spirit, it seems there are three verses of Scripture which indicate what a church can expect to have happen when the Holy Spirit is poured out upon them as a congregation:

First, the Spirit-filled church will become a witnessing church. Jesus said in Acts 1:8, "But ye shall receive power, after that the Holy Ghost is come upon you"—

—and you will be more *doctrinally sound* than any other church in town!

—and you will be more *rigid and unbending* in keeping the letter of the law!

—and you will *give more sacrificially* for world evangelism and missions.

—and you will enjoy greater moments of *emotional ecstasy.*

—and you will be *more committed* than anyone else to the old-fashioned ways.

All of these above suggestions on what happens when a church is filled with the Holy Spirit have been proclaimed with great vigor. They are good. But they are not scriptural. Churches need to be doctrinally sound, to live by the law, to give sacrificially to missions, to donate labor in the erection of a church, and to believe in the heritage of the church —but these are not the requisites given by Jesus Christ when He spoke to His disciples about the Spirit-filled life. Jesus made it perfectly clear that a person filled with the Holy Spirit would be a witness for Him.

"But ye shall receive power, after that the Holy Ghost is come upon you: *and ye shall be witnesses* unto me both in Jerusalem, and in all Judaea, and in Samaria, and unto the uttermost part of the earth" (Acts 1:8).

Many good people have done almost everything possible to find a suitable substitute for being witnesses. But it must be made clear that the New Testament indicates the very first requisite for being a Spirit-filled church is to become a witnessing congregation.

Witnessing may be organized with special nights, 3 x 5 cards, and all the paraphernalia, or it may be spontaneous. Witnessing may be tied to a bus program for reaching non-churched families in a community, or the church may not own a single bus. Witnessing may emphasize the marvelous experiences of young people going to Fort Lauderdale and other centers that attract college students, or it may be the less spectacular witnessing to a confused teen-ager in the local Sunday school class. But however the structure is put together, the church that is Spirit-filled will become totally a witnessing church in all it does from the pulpit on Sunday morning to the farthest off weekday activity.

And second, the Spirit-filled church will become a loving, caring fellowship of people. "But the fruit of the Spirit is *love,* joy, peace, longsuffering, gentleness, goodness, faith, meekness, temperance" (Gal. 5:22-23).

One Bible commentator has pointed out that the fruit of the Spirit is only one fruit. The verb form is singular. And the single fruit of the Spirit is love. From love comes joy. From love comes peace. From love comes long-suffering. From love comes gentleness. From love come goodness, meekness, temperance, and faith. But the root of every virtue is in love.

Dwight L. Moody ran a great Sunday school in Chicago. One cold January day a greeter stood at the front door to receive a latecomer who was a small, uncared-for boy. The youngster's cap was missing. His coat was too small and was held together at the neck with a safety pin. He wore no socks, and his shoes had belonged to someone else first. His legs were blue from the wind which came with numbing coldness off Lake Michigan.

Scooping the boy up into his arms, the man began rubbing the legs to encourage circulation. Standing him down at arm's length, the greeter asked, "Sonny, where do you live?"

The boy reported that he lived in a certain area which the greeter quickly calculated to be approximately two miles in one direction away from Moody's Sunday school. Surprised, he shot back, "Why did you do it? You must have gone by a dozen church doors this morning in order to come to Dwight L. Moody's Sunday school. Why did you walk over here in the cold this great distance in order to come to Sunday school?"

With the kind of honesty a boy has when he does not know a prepared answer but only gives the first thing that spontaneously comes to mind, the lad dropped open his jaw and said, "Sir, I guess it is because they understand a fellow over here."

That kind of love cannot be performed. It cannot be put on when it is not genuine. It is like sounding brass and tinkling cymbal if it is a performance rather than the genuine article. Furthermore, no one can legislate love. It cannot be put into the *Manual* or the rules of discipline. It comes from the heart of a person who has been filled with the Holy Spirit. And it also comes from the heart of the church that has been filled with the Holy Spirit.

Third, the church that has been filled with the Holy Spirit is possessed of an unbeatable optimism. "And be not drunk with wine, wherein is excess; but be filled with the Spirit . . . *making melody in your heart*" (Eph. 5:18-19).

The Bible says it was midnight when Paul and Silas sat in the depths of an old Philippian dungeon nursing the bruises on their backs and waiting for the next word in their destiny. I do not believe this was midnight on the clock. Clocks had not yet been invented. People used sundials. And sundials do not work at midnight. They work only in the sunshine. Therefore I believe this was midnight, the darkest hour emotionally and psychologically in this entire experience.

Paul and Silas, along with Dr. Luke and Timothy, had come across the Aegean Sea from the continent of Asia into Europe to proclaim the gospel. Among their converts was this teen-age girl who was making money for her managers by telling people about their future. One day she turned to the crowd and told them no longer to listen to her but to hear what Paul and Silas were saying, because these were men of God.

When Paul commanded the evil spirit to come out of the girl, she became clean, much to the anger of her managers. Paul and Silas were brought into a court which sentenced them to a Roman beating plus imprisonment. This beating was with the cruel Roman scourge, 39 times. These long leather thongs were woven with pieces of bone and metal which tore the flesh as the whipping was done across a man's back with a drawing motion.

Almost dead following their beating, Paul and Silas were cast into the old vermin-infested jail, where their hands and feet were secured in the stocks. As a Roman soldier marched on the cobblestones outside their iron door, Paul and Silas sat wondering what to do next, not knowing when the end might be.

If ever there were two men who could have sat in the midst of self-pity and felt like God and the people had forgotten them, it would have been Paul and Silas. However, during their midnight hour they did two things. *First, they began to pray.* This is not surprising because most people will pray when they get into a difficult situation. In the Orient these kinds of converts are called "rice Christians." In the army this kind of behavior is called "foxhole religion." But the prayers of Paul and Silas were different. I believe they prayed for God to bless Dr. Luke and Timothy, who had escaped this awful punishment. And anyone who stops to think about it knows that much more grace is needed to enjoy the successes of your friends than it does to comfort them during their hours of difficulty and tragedy. It takes much more of the grace of God to enjoy your friend's new automobile or new house than it does to comfort him when the car has been stolen and the house burned down. With the Holy Spirit in their lives, Paul and Silas had enough grace to pray a prayer of thanksgiving that things were no worse than they were, and that God had spared Dr. Luke and Timothy.

But second, the scripture also indicates that *Paul and Silas began to sing*. Many people can scarcely sing in the enthusiasm of a marvelous Sunday morning service, let alone in the darkest hours of life. There is no way to prove it, but I always have assumed that Paul was not a musician by nature. I doubt seriously if he could sing well enough to have his voice appreciated by those who listened. The melody was not a matter of vocal control, but a matter of a heart's condition. Because of the love of God and the optimism it produced within him, Paul, along with Silas, had a melody in his heart during the most difficult experiences of life.

Had Paul and Silas lived in our day, I believe they would have sung—

> *Must Jesus bear the cross alone,*
> *And all the world go free?*
> *No, there's a cross for everyone,*
> *And there's a cross for me.*

And I imagine they would have sung this—

> *Amazing grace! how sweet the sound!*
> *That saved a wretch like me!*
> *I once was lost, but now am found;*
> *Was blind, but now I see.*

And finally, I know they would have sung this verse in some kind of paraphrase that related directly to their situation—

> *Thro' many dangers, toils, and snares*
> *I have already come.*

> 'Tis grace hath brought me safe thus far,
> And grace will lead me home.

It does not take a lot of grace to be doctrinally sound. This can be achieved by enough study. It does not take a lot of grace to live by the letter of the law. Motivated more by the fear of God than by His love, many a person has made himself satisfied with the keeping of rules when he might have been set aglow with the additional dimension of the optimism of his love. It does not take a lot of grace to give sacrificially of time and money. Many people have been motivated to give sacrificially for causes that were totally unrelated to the kingdom of God. But it takes the grace of God poured out on individual lives and on the church as a total congregation for the spirit of optimism to dominate thoughts and decisions in the darkest hours of life's experiences.

The big question at this point is whether or not the Holy Spirit has been poured out recently upon your church. You can begin now to talk, teach, preach, pray, and sing about the coming of the Holy Spirit, knowing full well that this New Testament experience will transform a static, ingrown, little congregation into a marvelous witnessing, loving, caring, optimistic church.

CHAPTER 2

The Special Problems of Pastors and Lay Leaders

The devil does not die the day a man becomes pastor of a church or is elected a lay leader. In fact, it would seem logical Satan would be doubly diligent to destroy pastors and lay leaders. Since the thief does not go to the hovel to steal sterling silver but to the mansion on the hill, it is logical that the forces of evil would be pulled off the trail of a man committed to evil and used in every ambush possible to blow up the spiritual leadership of a pastor or lay leader.

The devil, however, does not attack leaders head on. He uses the most subtle approaches which cause the least alarm. Almost unnoticed, the wedge is driven in. The doorway is cracked open. Such problems are not unique to church personnel; but in a spiritual vocation in which the highest ethical standards prevail, the force of these problems seems greater than in the general population.

First, is the subtle problem of self-centeredness. Unless a minister is very careful in analyzing what is happening to him, the attitudes of those who love and appreciate him may tend to inflate his feelings concerning himself. Laymen often idealize or even pamper their minister. Business and professional people cater to clergy with ministerial discounts and other favors. Young ministers are often admired above and beyond the level of their growth and development. This fosters an inaccurate image of themselves and encourages behavior designed to produce great amounts of reassurance from others. In time this self-centeredness becomes obnoxious.

There are two ways this same problem of self-centeredness may develop in laymen. The person who plays a subordinate role in his secular work may find that his role of leadership and power among other laymen in the church is greater than he is accustomed to on the job. In fact, some laymen have tended to compensate for failure to achieve leadership in their regular secular work by becoming active leaders in the congregation.

Second, a man who is in a strong leadership position in his secular work may simply assume that he should have the same kind of role in the church. In either case, the danger is in the sly development of feelings of self-centeredness. And in either case, the result is a deterrent to spiritual growth.

Second is the problem of competition. Points of comparison with other pastors and lay leaders often show up in attendance records, finances, costs of building projects, and even more personal matters such as appointments to committees, prominent places on programs, and invitations to social functions. Among pastors, feelings of rejection may develop over failure to be appointed to certain places of service within the denominational structure. Even competition with other churches in the community or other churches within the denomination can become acute.

What is even more devastating is the possibility of competition developing between the pastor and his lay leaders. The pastor is head of the congregation but the layman's influence among members of the congregation usually has a longer history and thus is greater than the pastor's. If such competition develops, there is the possibility that "people manipulation" may take precedence over spiritual guidance.

Third is the problem of indolence. Neither the pastor nor the lay leader punches any kind of time clock at the church. What supervision there is must, by the nature of things, be very nebulous. There is no one, for example, to check if the pastor sleeps in, and no one to use leverage if the lay leader is guilty of irresponsibility in his assignment.

A pastor "working around the clock" can give the illusion of being very busy, when, really, a good day's work is not done. This leads to frustration, defensiveness, and guilt. He may be using the prime time of the day for doing errands for his wife or other personal assignments. Even time management can have spiritual overtones.

With both the layman and the pastor, the big problem is to determine the difference between what is urgent and what is important. Keeping up with the urgent can create a constant pressure which stops any significant attention to what is really important. At the same time, a lack of hobbies or secondary interests can cause the primary life purpose to become perfunctory, and one's calling to become a duty.

Fourth is the problem of personal money matters. Pastors, who by tradition are low on the salary scale, may tend to nurse their grievances and blame lay leaders. Lay leaders, on the other hand, may feel the pastor is adequately paid by the layman's own standards of income and wonder why the clergyman appears to be a money-oriented man. Among either ministers or laymen, living beyond one's income is disastrous to spiritual leadership. The pastor or layman who cannot handle his own personal finances probably will not do well with the finances of the church either.

Fifth is the problem of public scrutiny. Physical appearance is always on parade for the pastor and his wife, even when it is not supposed to be. Many persons impose a perfectionist standard upon the pastor and his family in matters of conduct, attitude, and appearance. The residents of the parsonage cannot be protected from the public scrutiny both inside the church and outside. And the moment a layman becomes a leader in the congregation, his own privacy has, to a degree, been sacrificed. A Sunday school superintendent, head usher, finance chairman, or other lay leader in the church, must expect to carry his role with him wherever he goes and in whatever things he does. He is not a lay leader on Sundays only. A pastor is a pastor, and a lay leader is a lay leader all day and all night, seven days and nights per week.

Sixth is the problem of criticism. Criticism is universal. When the pastor first assumes his role, he exposes himself and his family to the critical eye and tongue of all who are interested. And whenever a lay leader stands to his feet, lifts his voice, or takes a step forward, he exposes himself to the possibility of criticism.

Even worse than criticism is unfounded rumor. Dr. George Alport says that a rumor equals the degree of interest people have in a person or thing multiplied by the lack of accurate information available. So if the people are especially interested in what the pastor is doing and they have no information about the coming and going in various levels of his family activity, the rumor factory will begin to grind out erroneous information. The real problem is whether or not a pastor or lay leader has enough of the power of the Holy Spirit to absorb unfair criticism. Do not cry, "Unfair!"

when you are criticized as a leader in the local church. This goes with the assignment. The real challenge is to have enough internal strength to absorb the blow.

Seventh is the problem of an unclear goal. The challenge of the New Testament is to preach the gospel to every creature of every nation. But no one person or church can fulfill this challenge alone. Since it is unclear exactly how much the church should be doing, some churches go without any definite goals. Both the pastor and lay leaders define their own goals and then try to persuade others to share in them. The goals must be realistic, attainable, and must make sense to all who are going to share them. Effective leadership begins with a clear-cut goal, and the breakdown in leadership begins at the point in which goals are unclear or lack challenge. Periodic reprogramming of one's own goals and purposes is one of the most difficult problems facing the pastor and the lay leader.

Eighth is the problem of emotional isolation. Although this pertains more to the pastor than to the lay leader, it is really a problem which both kinds of leaders share. Every pastor needs a pastor, but very few have anyone to whom they can turn. And emotional isolation tends to develop unsatisfactory emotions. Paranoia can develop, which causes one to have a persecution complex, to see problems where there are none, to find shadows in the sunshine, and feel that he is misunderstood and unappreciated. Anxiety, which begins with a fear of failure, may be diffused to cover every aspect of life.

This type of pastor or lay leader projects the feeling of being harassed, that too much is demanded of him, that he is unable to fulfill the expectations of the people. Ultimately, this kind of anxiety can lead to a crippling fear of failure in which one does not attempt anything which involves risk. The only antidote to this emotional isolation is a worthwhile Christian fellowship with at least one other individual plus a meaningful devotional life day by day.

These problems, or hang-ups, must be faced by every pastor and lay leader, or a combination of more serious defects will develop. The above eight problems in themselves are not serious. But unless an inner spiritual strength can be developed to take these in stride or make necessary corrections, there is a high possibility that one of the following four very serious kinds of problems will result.

Among pastors and lay leaders, the most serious and common spiritual defect is resentment. Resentment toward real or imagined competitors will be destructive to any kind of spiritual life. Lay leaders may resent pastoral leadership, or pastors may resent lay leaders. There can be resentment toward church administrators, such as superintendents, bishops, or other persons in high position. Unless the problem of resentment is brought into focus, an unhealthy attitude of cynicism can result. And cynicism among religious people often takes the form of believing that everything in the church is manipulated. The power of God is sublimated, if not almost forgotten, while human explanations are substituted for divine sovereignty.

Closely related to resentment is the devastating problem of self-pity. Pastors and lay leaders who have allowed themselves to become resentful usually develop attitudes of self-pity toward themselves and their assignments. Self-pity is a way of thinking about oneself. It is not necessarily related to circumstances. It has nothing to do basically with the way things are. It is a way of thinking about one's own assignment in comparison with other people's lot in life. The man who has allowed himself to develop resentment will almost always feel that other pastors, other lay leaders, or other persons, whoever they may be, have a better situation than his own. Because of this, a ceiling of impregnable negativism develops around and over the church, blocking spiritual growth and development. Nothing is more destructive than attitudes of self-pity.

Hidden sin becomes a way out for some men who are frustrated by their hang-ups. Unable to deal successfully with their minor problems such as self-centeredness, competition, money matters, public scrutiny, criticism, and emotional isolation, many men will seek to alleviate their pressures through some immoral relationship. Ordinarily there are three kinds of hidden sin: (1) sex immorality, (2) stealing, and (3) a deceptive life.

The best antidote to developing an immoral relationship in any area of life is to pray for enough wisdom and judgment to stop at the very beginning of any such temptation. A girl wrote Ann Landers protesting the criticisms of her friends who found fault with her because she would usually end a lovely evening with her boyfriend by spending a couple of hours alone with him in her apartment. Feeling unfairly criticized, she asked the question, "Do you think I did wrong?" Ann Landers' answer was in one word, "Probably!"

Sin does not happen in a vacuum. A set of circumstances begin to develop out of which sinful behavior becomes the natural result. The pastor or lay leader who sees any kind of situation developing out of which sinful conduct might evolve must take whatever drastic steps are necessary to change the situation radically. If he doesn't, there will be a tragic catastrophe. If possible, help must be sought on both the spiritual and psychological aspects of the problem which motivates this kind of behavior. Also, remember the "rules of the game" as set down on tablets of stone on Mount Sinai. They are as real and binding today as they were then.

The final result of failure to cope with the stresses of the ministry or the assignment of a lay leader is the development of a depressing negativism. The human mind is like the computer which receives into it all the impulses that are a part of its experience. And like any computer, the only response the human being can give to any experience is either a plus factor or a minus factor. The data is interpreted either positively and in its best light or negatively and in its worst light. No person or situation is entirely good or bad. All of life is a mixture of good and bad.

A negative person looks at the situation and sees only the bad, negative things, while the positive individual looks at the same situation and sees all of its good possibilities. An effective pastor is never a negative person. There never was a negative-thinking champion. But many a church has been stifled beyond the power of the Holy Spirit to change the atmosphere because the pastoral and/or lay leadership of the congregation was basically negative in its outlook on life.

But what can be done for one who is already trapped by his own problems until the fruits of resentment, self-pity, hidden sin, and negativism have taken over and dominated him?

It is not hopeless!

1. *To begin with, the road toward help starts by facing oneself squarely.* The problem is not theological, but spiritual; not denominational, but personal; not the fault of the ministry, but of oneself. The easiest thing in the world to do is for one to find a scapegoat for his failures in pastoral or lay leadership. The superintendency, the denominational headquarters, and the Christian college are the most popular of all these scapegoats. But one is not responsible for the problems which accompany the ministry; he is responsible for his reaction to them. Admit those feelings frankly.

"But be ye doers of the word, and not hearers only, deceiving your own selves. For if any be a hearer of the word, and not a doer, he is like unto a man beholding his natural face in a glass: for he beholdeth himself, and goeth his way, and straightway forgetteth what manner of man he was" (Jas. 1:22-24).

2. *Admit and discuss one's feelings ·freely with some non-judgmental person in whom he has confidence.* God has given pastors and lay leaders the capacity to gain insight into their own problems when these problems may be articulated freely in the presence of a non-judgmental person. Since there is a tendency in the church to major on weaknesses instead of strengths, many tend to hide their problems instead of admit and discuss them. There is a fear that an admission of need may be a demonstration of weakness. But the fact is that more and more people are coming to realize that every man needs a person with whom he may talk freely about his own spiritual pilgrimage.

3. *Try to trace back the problem to its original source, as nearly as possible.* For instance, jealousy which grew out of feelings of competition might be traced back to an unfortunate event in a church-sponsored contest of some earlier day. Or resentment might be traced back to a slight or hurt given by a person on whom you had always depended. As best you can, trace back the troublesome problems to their original source.

4. *Finally, pray for forgiveness and seal the forgiveness with a new commitment.* Among my friends is a lay leader who uses every Saturday of the year to clean out his own spiritual problems. If someone has hurt him, criticized him severely, or done some other thing which has left its mark, this gentleman sees to it that everything is cleared up in his own mind before he assumes his Sunday responsibilities in the church. He has indicated that this weekly habit of clearing out the spiritual cobwebs and "skeletons" has been a source of great spiritual strength to him over a period of many years.

Bishop Cushman, confronted by his own spiritual deterioration, came to a point of absolute frustration in the church where he served. He prostrated himself on the floor of his study and there, over a period of hours, he wrestled with himself and the problems that had caused him to become spiritually sidetracked. Finally, as he reports, "At about three o'clock on that Sunday afternoon, I came to the place of forgiveness and new commitment. And there on my face I made a promise to God that never again as long as I live would I take into my body physical food on any day until first I had received spiritual food into my soul."

A Saturday cleaning of the cobwebs, or a great traumatic experience like Bishop Cushman's, may not be everyone's way of dealing spiritually with the problems; but if a church is to be transformed, all of the spiritual roadblocks and pipeline debris must be cleaned out. Then and only then can one be ready to become a spiritual leader, as either pastor or layman, in the church.

CHAPTER 3

How a Pastor Becomes
a Leader

The Early Church did not just grow; it was organized in its own way. Within the 12 apostles there was the inner circle of Peter, James, and John, who might be described as the lay decision-makers. In the first chapter of Acts, the election of Matthias to take the place of Judas was important enough for Dr. Luke to record the event. In the sixth chapter of Acts, considerable attention is given to the election of the first church board of seven men. And the first general assembly of the Early Church, held in Jerusalem, is recorded in the fifteenth chapter of Acts. On that occasion there was a key issue on which the apostles and certain leaders in the Jerusalem church clashed. James was the moderator. A final vote resulted in a paper which was signed and sent to the congregations in the north by Silas and Judas Barsabas. On another occasion, in an area meeting in Antioch, Paul "withstood . . . [Peter] to the face."

And certainly, no one can deny that the Early Church had strong leadership in Peter, an articulate, forceful, converted fisherman. And in the Apostle Paul the Church had a well-educated, cosmopolitan, open-minded preacher, theologian, missionary, and church administrator. The Scriptures indicate that Timothy was handpicked and trained for the specific role of a church leader. This leads to the following conclusion: *Competent pastoral leadership over a period of years is the first answer to the problem of transforming a small church.* There are several ways the Spirit helps a pastor become a leader.

The Holy Spirit will help a man answer for himself the three basic questions of life. Unless these three questions are answered, nothing else really matters much. These are basic to every pastor and lay leader who is to become an effective person. They are as follows:

What kind of person am I? This is the central theme of self-image psychology. What is the picture I have of my strengths and weaknesses? What am I really like in the inner man? Having firm answers to these questions is the only adequate defense against criticism in the pastorate. If the pastor or lay leader does not know who he is, then any kind of criticism which floats back to him second- or third-hand will be demoralizing. It usually results in his lashing back against those who have originated the criticism, accusing them of gross unfairness. Answering this first basic question is the initial step in personal growth and development.

Where am I going? All of the little questions are suddenly answered when this issue is settled. The penalty for failing to answer this question is eventual boredom and often cynicism. If the sails aren't set, the ship drifts. The first six months in any new pastorate may well be spent in trying to determine one or two specific goals toward which the pastor feels everything in the ministry of this church must be turned. The simplest sort of goal is a new piece of church property and/or a new building. The most difficult kind of goal is the changing of a set of attitudes in a church that has bogged down numerically and spiritually. The goal might be the long-term financing for a congregation which has over-extended itself in debt. Organizing a new church, or filling up an empty one, or demonstrating the possibility of growth in a difficult spot, might all be suitable answers to the question, Where am I going?

Why am I doing what I am doing? It is marvelous for any pastor to feel that the place he serves is exactly where he belongs in God's will at this time. This settles the question of freedom and fulfillment within the denominational framework. If the place I am serving now is the place where I am willing to spend the rest of my life, then there is no need to be looking over the fence for greener pastures, or doing a job with one eye cast on another possible assignment.

The Holy Spirit will help a man to become sensitive to the needs people feel. The first test of sensitivity to the needs of people comes in the preparation of sermons. A lot of time is wasted in answering questions no one is asking. For years I followed a system of self-discipline in which I offered to provide copies of sermons for the people of the congregation and their friends as they were asked for. I found that preaching on some themes brought a courteous remark about the weather as people shook hands with me on their way out the door. Other kinds of themes which were related directly to the problems the people were facing in daily life always resulted in a request for copies of the message.

The same approach is true in planning church services on Sunday mornings and Sunday evenings. No one needs to be urged to attend a service which meets several different needs people in the family feel. If the music is inspirational, the sermon helpful, and the fellowship therapeutic, then people in increasing numbers will be interested in attending the church. But if informality is a way of covering up for unpreparedness, and exhortations on the "oughts" and "shoulds" become substitutes for well-planned, Spirit-filled sermons, and if people show little interest in each other, the seats in the church will become increasingly available.

The same concept of meeting the needs people feel relates directly to the kinds of programs the church sponsors. No organization, committee, tradition, or procedure deserves to be supported that does not meet people's needs. For instance, almost any church can double its Wednesday night attendance by planning activities to meet the needs of all age-groups in the family.

And finally, this concept of sensitivity to the needs of people is absolutely basic in personal relationships. A pastor or evangelist who is more sensitive to his own feelings than those of others had better be kept away from the people as persons. Loving crowds is quite different from loving people. Seeing the people as pockets or statistics is quite different from seeing them as objects of service.

The Holy Spirit will help a man become an authentic person. Small children are beautiful because they are open and transparent. But as boys and girls grow up they begin to learn that it is not always wise to say what you think, or express what you feel. You may get slapped down and punished. By the time people become adults, everyone takes it for granted that there is an outward, performing self which is put on display for people to see and a more genuine, real self that is kept concealed. People who are adept at this game can hide their inner feelings until even the husband or wife with whom they live does not really know how they think and feel.

In some vocations the two selves may be quite acceptable. But in ministering to the needs of people, the only person who can really be helpful is the man of God who is authentic through and through. The performing self must be in direct focus with the inner man. A lost soul walking around on earth is the man who has been estranged from his real self for so many years he has forgotten who he was. All he is, is a person performing a role. A stained-glass voice, a set of perfected techniques, or a well-stored reservoir of old clichés does not make for a man of God. The pastor or layman who is going to be a useful leader must become an authentic person. The highest compliment Jesus ever gave any man was concerning Nathanael, of whom He said, "Behold an Israelite indeed, in whom is no guile!" (John 1:47)

The Holy Spirit will help a man to develop a style of leadership that brings out the best in people. Basically, there are three kinds of leadership:

First is the authoritarian pastor or lay leader. This person tries to manipulate and force people to his own will, assuming his judgment is best for everyone. Manipulation, bending people to one's own will against their wishes, has been thoroughly tried at many times and places in man's history, and it does not work—at least not for long. Manipulation of people by an authoritarian approach is sometimes done under the guise of a great, patriarchal sovereign, or may be more openly demonstrated as that of a little tyrant, or even as a contrived demonstration of love. But the facade is seldom sufficient to keep people confused for long. The nature of the world in which we live does not now easily accept church leadership which is akin to military dictatorship.

Other pastors and lay leaders try the *laissez-faire* approach. This French word simply means, "Hands off." This kind of pastor becomes the executive secretary of the board. He does not project programs and lay out plans. He simply tries to find out what the church board wants and then does it. Such a person is hardly worthy of a leadership role.

The really productive and useful pastor or lay leader is the man with the *democratic way of working with people.* This leader tries to show the people what they can do, and by various ways release the potential ability of the church board to outline and execute a forward-looking set of policies and plans. The democratic pastor believes that the source of authority is the experience and vision of all those concerned in the operation of the church. He makes his ideas and plans explicit, so others can give him relevant information.

Another way of explaining these three kinds of leadership is given in the symbols of plus and minus. Examine the chart on attitudes of leadership.

ATTITUDES	
TOWARD SELF	TOWARD OTHERS
+ − +	− + +

The plus or minus figure in the left-hand column stands for a leader's attitude toward himself. And the plus or minus in the right-hand column stands for his attitudes toward the people he works with.

The plus-minus pastor has strong attitudes toward his own ability and power while he has very poor attitudes concerning the ability of his colleagues. This kind of pastor does not trust lay leadership. Or this kind of lay leader does not trust pastoral leadership. He is eager to keep control of all that happens. Ordinarily, a plus-minus leader will do a great job over a short period of time, reversing the statistical trend in the sales organization, the Sunday school class, the church, the district, or wherever it may be. But a plus-minus man often becomes a whizbang. He is a whiz one year and a bang the next. The tenure of a plus-minus person is short, usually not more than two years. In a Sunday school class it may be only a few months. For in pushing his own ideas, the plus-minus person tends to bulldoze other people, leaving enough scars in his wake to create problems that eventually erode his leadership.

The minus-plus pastor, on the other hand, is a man with very weak concepts concerning himself, but very strong appreciation for the skills of others. This kind of leader is forever trying to secure one more study from an expert before he does anything. This kind of person always wants a committee to make a study. He covers up his tracks before they are made. He never makes decisions fully on his own and therefore frustrates those who are unhappy with his leadership because it is difficult to find him in wrong judgment. This kind of person often becomes very secure in an institutional-type relationship. He never gets anything done, but he doesn't make mistakes.

The final and best kind of leader in the church is the *plus-plus pastor or layman*. This kind of individual has great confidence in his own skills but has an equal confidence in the skills and abilities of others. He looks to people for the kinds of work they are able to do and puts his trust in them as well as in himself. This man can work productively in an assignment over a period of many years. And it is likely that the saddest day in the church where he serves will be the day that he announces his resignation to take on a bigger assignment in another place.

There is still another way to diagram leadership in the church. Many organizations try to make charts which start with the leader and those who are immediately responsible to him plus all the other individuals serving underneath these persons. This is called a line-and-staff operation. This is the way the army is run. Rulings are handed down from above and follow the line down to the last buck private. Staff personnel not in the line are only in an advisory relationship and never have any power, because people who are taught to think in channels will take orders from the person in authority and ignore the help of the staff person who may be more knowledgeable and better qualified.

A much better approach to diagramming authority and leadership in a local church is given in the figure of the circle. Examine the chart which indicates how a church may make decisions. The problem or challenge of the moment is cast into the very center of the ring. Around the ring are gathered all of the persons who might have pertinent information to help in making a good decision on ways to meet the challenge or alleviate the problem. No one is concerned about who is to get the credit. Leadership shifts from one person to another quickly as different kinds of information are needed. The pastor's role is that of a resource person to guide and direct the discussion but not to dominate it. Thus, his leadership is not threatened; he does not take opposition to his ideas personally, and does not feel a strong motivation to win or save face.

The personnel resources for solving problems

The Holy Spirit will help a man learn to lead people to change in acceptable ways. The three traditional ways to break resistance are: (1) Be the king of the mountain; (2) Tell the people to do what they already want to do; (3) Gain confidence and invoke minor changes, steering the board toward greater changes on the basis of success in the minor ones.

Actually none of the above ways to effect change is good for long. Decisions in the process of change must always involve the people who are to undergo the change. They must be involved in planning, in learning to understand the problem, and in choosing one or more of the options which are available. A set of radical changes may be wrought inside a congregation in a fairly short time by following three simple procedures: (1) Get an accurate picture of the present situation as it really is, securing this information in a manner that will help all of the congregation to agree that this is the way things are. (2) Use the lay leaders of the church in painting a crystal-clear picture of what can be accomplished. And then (3) help the people to see clearly the steps necessary to fill in the picture of what can be. *Any dream which can be visualized by the pastor and shared by the congregation can become reality.* But if the pastor does not have a clear picture of what the church can become, he has nothing to share with the congregation, and often the result is a nightmare.

The Holy Spirit helps a man develop the team concept. A reading of the New Testament reveals immediately that the Early Church leaders worked in teams. They were not loners. Paul had with him Timothy, Luke, and Silas. And in each church he founded there was evidence of team leadership.

The modern pastoral assignment is too big and too complicated for any one man. The pastor is expected to be a specialist in preaching, fund raising, administration, Christian education, music, counseling, visitation, children's work, teen programs, and any number of other kinds of useful endeavors. Of course, it is impossible for him to fill all these roles adequately. The pastor who will become a real leader in the church learns how to work through other people in developing a team capable of dealing with all the challenges the church faces.

It is not necessary for a staff in the church to receive salary. Even in a very small church the pastor can develop around him a team of people who are capable of multiplying his time and energies manyfold. One of the best men I ever knew served as the pastor's lay assistant in the church for seven years without pay. As a retired store manager, he added dignity to the service by reading the Scriptures every Sunday morning and by visiting personally in the homes of all the new people who attended the church. In a seven-year period he called in more than 4,500 homes. He even bought his own gasoline. To this man, who became the first member of a pastor's team, was added a children's visitor who functioned in a similar assignment, only with boys and girls. To these there could be added a specialist in music and volunteer help in the church office.

Even in a church of fewer than 50 members, the pastor can be assisted by a person in charge of the work of boys and girls, another in charge of teen activities, and a third in charge of adult programs. Add to these a helper in music, and the team is on its way to an expanded ministry. Even if there are no teen-agers to serve, a teen director can be appointed and the teen-agers recruited. But the pastor who feels he must be the center of all the activity, doing all the work himself, is limited in the size of the congregation he can build and serve.

The principles involved in setting up effective team structure are as follows: (1) Laymen respond to a clear-cut responsibility which demands a reasonable amount of service from them. (2) Responsibility for any assignment must be accompanied with commensurate authority to do the job. (If responsibility and authority are divided, then nothing but frustration results.) (3) The pastor must be a specialist in giving recognition and credit for work well done.

The Holy Spirit helps a man to learn that nothing is impossible which can be visualized. The best definition of faith in the Bible is the first verse of Hebrews 11: "Now faith is the substance of things hoped for, the evidence of things not seen." This means that faith visualizes the things hoped for; it sees things like they can be. And second, faith begins to act as though this vision of things which can be will actually become real. To visualize what can be done is the mark of a great pastoral leader. And the great lay leader is the man who can catch this vision with the pastor and start conducting the affairs of the church as though this vision is actually going to become reality. The walls of Jericho came tumbling down, not because of a new technology developed by the children of Israel, but because of obedience to a mental picture. This principle of faith as belief in mental pictures can be applied equally to the erection of new church buildings and to the development of new programs and the necessary personnel to meet the needs of the growing congregation. God helps a leader to see what *can* be done and then helps him to guide the people in believing it *will* be done.

Before this chapter on pastoral leadership is closed, something needs to be said about the word "charisma." This is supposed to be a magic quality held by men of great leadership ability. Men like Billy Graham, Dr. Norman Vincent Peale, and many other religious leaders have an unusual something about them which seems to draw people magnetically. But the best thing for a pastor of a local church to do concerning charisma is to forget it. He can rejoice in those men who have this great quality, but he must not feel defeated because he does not. Most of God's workers come from the rank and file of ordinary people.

The purpose of this book, and the purpose of the ministry among both pastors and laymen, is to understand more fully the practical ways in which human energy may be organized for expanding the kingdom of God. Many young men with a certain amount of charisma have become dismal failures, discarded along the way, because they found the results too easy and did not apply themselves diligently in preparation and hard work. Many of these men who today are out of the ministry or places of lay leadership were shipwrecked on the beautiful coral reefs of easy initial success.

The giant of a leader is the man who has a combination of charisma, hard work, good preparation, and an understanding of people. However, these persons are few and far between. It is not for you and me to be concerned about them. God has built His kingdom with millions of ordinary people and only a handful of leadership giants. Let us leave the giants to themselves while we give our energies to developing whatever potential God has given us to lead the people in the place where we serve.

THE PASTOR
AND THE
CHURCH BOARD

CHAPTER 4

Choosing the
Church Board

It is a generally accepted fact that back of every great man are the power and strength of a good woman.

It is equally true that back of every effective pastor are the power and strength of a good church board.

It also may be said that back of every effective, growing church are the power and strength of a pastor and a church board who work together in providing the motivating force for the entire congregation.

The converse may be stated, that the "beginning of the end" is at hand when any pastor and church board cease to be a motivating force for each other and for the congregation, or when they begin to turn their energies to internal conflicts.

The first precedent for organizing the church comes from Jesus himself. His was a very informal, unstructured type of ministry. He had no buildings encumbered by mortgages. There was no parsonage, no church kitchen, no office with clacking typewriters and rumbling mimeographs. There was no manual of operation, no annual meeting, no Sunday school, youth organization—not even a missionary society. He preached on the hillsides, in homes, and on the steps of the Temple. He slept in the open or in the homes of friends. And He had but 12 official members of His church. But even at that, Jesus had the basic elements of an organization. To begin with, He was the undisputed Leader. In addition, there was a treasurer, and a three-man executive committee. Even the 12 must have considered themselves the nucleus for a greater organization to come, because Luke records in detail the Upper Room election of Matthias to take the place of Judas.

The expansion of this organization to include an official church board took place very early in the history of the Church. Here is the background, from Acts 6:3: "Wherefore, brethren, look ye out among you seven men of honest report, full of the Holy Ghost and wisdom, whom we may appoint over this business."

The Jews in Jerusalem at Pentecost were of two types. There were Jews who lived in Palestine. They spoke Hebrew and Aramaic, were fixed in the historic traditions, and were firmly attached to the soil of the Holy Land. They developed feelings of superiority over foreign Jews and looked with shriveling disdain on Samaritans and on all Gentiles.

The other type of Jew lived outside the Holy Land. His ancestral roots were outside Palestine for generations past. He had long since forgotten Aramaic and Hebrew, if ever he knew it. He spoke fluent Greek, the commercial language of the Mediterranean world. He was much more cosmopolitan than his Palestinian counterpart, and much more tolerant of Gentile ideas. These Jews lived in what is now North Africa, Egypt, Iraq, Iran, Turkey, Greece, Syria, and Italy. (A list of these nations is given in the second chapter of Acts.)

Now the Jewish synagogue had a kindly tradition of caring for its families suffering temporary hardship. Each Friday there were two officials of the synagogue who visited each house for alms and goods. This fund was called "The Basket" because of the receptacle used in its collection. In addition, there were daily visits to the homes for money to give those in pressing need. This fund was called "The Tray."

The Early Church, which borrowed many ideas from the synagogue, wisely took up the custom of helping its own needy members. But during the first days of the Church trouble arose between the Hebrew Jewish-Christians and the Grecian Jewish-Christians over the handling of these funds. The Hebrews found it very difficult to give their alms for the needs of those Jews who spoke Greek and were not really Palestinian. A mental roadblock developed. As a result there arose a murmuring among the Grecian widows that they were either inadvertently or deliberately being left out of the daily distribution of money and food to the needy.

The apostles saw that secular demands on their time would leave them with no energy or opportunity to do their main spiritual business, so they asked the people to elect seven men who became the first church board. The purpose of this seven-man board was to quiet the murmurings among the people by effectively dealing with the secular problems of the church and thus free the ministry to do its spiritual work more effectively.

May I say, parenthetically, that I take the word "men" to be generic. This does not indicate women should not serve on the board. Actually, there are several reasons why there should be some board representation among the women:

1. Women often have special spiritual sensitivities beyond their male counterparts.

2. Women often have a special awareness of the problems of children in the congregation.

3. Women have special skills or aptitudes in such areas as music, aesthetics, Sunday school needs, and kitchen operation.

4. Women often bring unique ideas or perspectives to the board which are foreign to the thinking of men.

5. Women often have more time for follow-through and implementation of board business than do the men.

But back to the first church board. There are at least two useful observations concerning its structure and operation:

The Kinds of Persons Who Were Elected

These members were "men of honest report." A good reputation is a highest priority for a board member. The writer of Proverbs believed that a good name is rather to be chosen than great riches (22:1). And in Paul's greeting to the Romans he said with great joy, "Your faith [or your reputation] is spoken of throughout the whole world" (1:8). But it was Jesus who said it best. Concerning reputation, He said, "Let your light so shine before men, that they may see your good works, and glorify your Father which is in heaven" (Matt. 5:16).

There was once a church board member in our church who owned a large dairy serving the entire city from door to door and in grocery stores. He wanted to expand his business by adding the food services of a large auto plant. After submitting his bid he was called in by the purchasing agent and all but asked outright for an under-the-table kickback. When it was evident he would not cooperate in any such nefarious scheme, the purchasing agent signed the order contract and shook hands with my board member, saying, "Had you agreed to a bribe, I would not have given you the business. For if you had done unethical things to get the business, you would not have hesitated to do other questionable things to increase your profit." His reputation and his profit were increased simultaneously by this stand on conscience. And, incidentally, both these increases made him a more useful member of the church board.

But another qualification of these early board members

was that they were to be men full of the Holy Ghost. The New Testament indicates there is a difference between having the Holy Spirit and being filled with the Holy Spirit. It is the fullness of the Spirit which is needed by board members. Jesus knew the kinds of problems the Early Church would face. This is why He told His followers to stay in Jerusalem until they were filled with the Holy Spirit. The apostles must have had foresight into the kinds of situations the first church board would face. Therefore they charged the people that men be chosen who were filled with the Holy Ghost.

Those who are filled with the Spirit are going to be faithful to all services of the church. Theirs is the kind of faithfulness which makes everyone know in the event of absence that there is illness or some other acceptable reason for their having missed. In stewardship they accept the biblical plan of tithing as a base. The Spirit-filled ones carry spiritual responsibility at home and in church. Perhaps most of all, they are characterized by an attitude of love, the capacity to enjoy people like they are instead of the way they wish they were.

The apostles further charged the people to elect men who were full of wisdom. Paul, in his letter to Titus, indicates that wisdom is evidenced in the man who is able to rule his own home and his own spirit. "Ordain elders in every city, as I had appointed thee: if any be blameless, the husband of one wife, having faithful children not accused of riot or unruly. For a bishop must be blameless, as the steward of God; not selfwilled, not soon angry, not given to wine, no striker, not given to filthy lucre; but a lover of hospitality, a lover of good men, sober, just, holy, temperate" (1:5-8).

Without doing harm to the intent of the text, it might be made to apply to a church board member today. It means, in summary, that a man who evidences wisdom in ruling his own spirit, his own home, and his own business is a good risk for exercising wisdom in church affairs. Conversely, the man who is not able to deal effectively with his own personal problems will not likely use good wisdom in handling the problems of the church.

And finally, the apostles charged the people to choose men who were full of faith.

There have been churches whose pastor-church board relationship was not unlike the relationship of a jury and the prosecuting attorney. The board sits in rows as in a jury box, and the pastor stands before them to present his case like a prosecuting attorney. When the pastor has finished the case for his ideas, the church board jury votes thumbs-up or thumbs-down. And it is to the pastor's advantage to be right 51 percent of the time, at least. In this approach the board sees its chief function as granting or withholding permission for the pastor to do the things he wants to do while the pastor sees his role as getting ideas "past" the board so he can implement them.

In this relationship, the pastor perceives the board as a roadblock to progress, and the board views the pastor as a revolutionary who is intent on changing everything. The board, then, is accused of being conservative and the pastor is considered visionary. Part of the board goes along with the pastor, wanting to give him a free hand in everything, and the other part holds securely to the reins of authority. The board and the pastor then burn up all their spiritual energies on each other, while the devil laughs at a church which stops growing and becomes more ingrown with each passing year.

We must see, then, the four characteristics the apostles thought most important for membership on the church board: these seven men were to be (1) men of good reputation, (2) filled with the Holy Spirit, (3) full of wisdom, and (4) full of faith.

What Happened When This Group Took Over Their Assignments

First, "the word of God increased." When the apostles were relieved of many secular duties, they gave themselves more fully to the highest priority, the Word of God. One of the biggest problems a pastor faces is the control of his expenditure of time and energy so that he can concentrate on the more important matters. The board of the Early Church was wise in that it arranged for the secular matters and the mechanics of the enterprise, while the apostles gave themselves more fully to the preaching and teaching of the Word.

Second, the number of the disciples increased and a number of the priests were converted. This means the church grew. There are two reasons for this growth. One is the strange and wonderful chemistry which seems to operate when the pastor and the board work well together. The other is the factor already mentioned, that the apostles were able to concentrate on their ministry of the Word.

One last observation concerning this first election of a board is that the first martyr in the Christian Church was from this number, not from among the apostles. This man whose wisdom and spirit they could not resist was a board member. This man who had a face which shone like an angel was a trustee of the church. This man who was stoned to death was Stephen, a voting member of the official church board.

It is not the easiest job in the world to serve on the church board. There are no actual stonings these days, but pressures mount and sometimes become acute. It is disappointing to see some people explode under pressure, but there is a great inner satisfaction in watching those who, under similar pressure, evidence a spirit nobody can gainsay. I've not seen any board members whose faces shone like angels, but I've seen them hold steady with an inner composure which could not be explained outside the power of the Spirit.

CHAPTER 5

The Behavior of
Church Board Members

Almost at the end of my graduate program, I petitioned the academic committee for permission to do a directed study under the chairman of the Sociology Department of the university. After an expression of general agreement, the chairman of the committee asked me what I wanted to study. When I told him that I was interested in doing research on the behavior of church board members, the entire group burst into hilarious laughter.

But I went on to explain to them that I was dead serious. The discussion of board members in churches and Christian colleges had been a frequent subject of dinner-table conversation in the home where I grew up. And anyone who observes persons on official boards is forced to conclude that they often behave differently in the various situations.

Granted permission from the committee, I began to gather a bibliography of primary sources. The sociology chairman said that I could read only the reports on original research rather than books that had been written on the basis of research done by somebody else. Three months later

I presented to him a 70-page paper. In the final paragraph I said that, on the basis of research, *it is impossible to predict in advance the behavior of any board member in a given situation.* I always have thought it was because of this final sentence that I received a high mark on this paper.

But, regardless of the unpredictability of board members in any given situation, there are some very definite clues which will help a pastor or lay leader to understand more fully why board members behave the way they do in official sessions.

1. *The first clue is the power structure.* Maybe a better term than power structure is decision makers. But regardless of what it is called, there is a small group whose decisions make a difference to all the rest. In any church board meeting members tend to address themselves to a few people, for these are the ones whose feelings and reactions they care about. Dr. Thelen, at the University of Chicago, says that this inner group on a board of 20 members is never larger than eight and often much smaller.

It is just a fact of life that people organized together officially always develop an inner group of decision makers. In the United States Senate chamber, the two seats in the front row on either side of the center aisle are occupied by some very powerful men. Although there are more than 100 men in the Senate, it is doubtful if anyone could ever push though a bill these four men opposed. It is a small group of men who are the power structure. One person in a high office in Washington said that many Americans would not sleep well if they knew how few men actually make the decisions which run the country.

In the church this group of decision makers can be a center of grave frustration and difficulty for the pastor. If he is not able to live in harmony with them and profit by their usefulness in decision making, they are likely to be looked upon as church bosses and stereotyped as carnal. Some years ago

I pulled into the driveway of a pastor friend of mine who came out the door and started talking to me before I got out of the car about the church bosses in his congregation. He finally said, "I have decided to dedicate one year of my life to get rid of these men who have blocked progress all these years." Without saying so to him, I made a mental note to watch and see what happened. Six months later he had moved out of the parsonage and was working as a carpenter —out of the ministry. And the same decision-making group is still in the church working well with a man who understands and appreciates them.

Even if a decision-making group in the congregation could be destroyed in one stroke of lightning, another power structure would evolve before the next meeting of the church board. The board members who have power may use it flagrantly or unobtrusively, in small or in great measure, but it will be used. The pastor might as well accept this fact and learn how to live with them.

The really serious problem in a church board is the possibility of conflict between two competing power structures. The twin feelings of cooperation and competition are rarely missing on a church board. This ambivalence will reflect itself from issue to issue. The communication of ideas, coordination of efforts, friendliness, and pride in one's group which are basic to board harmony and effectiveness are disrupted when competition develops among the decision makers. The pastor, in particular, is in grave trouble if he is caught between the conflicts of two decision-making groups who compete with each other for power, even though he may not personally be the subject of controversy.

Some church board members become a part of the power structure because of their personal dedication to the church; others, by vocational or financial status; some, by demonstrated competence; others, by personal qualities; and still others, because they are designated persons of authority.

But regardless of the source, the fact of a power structure is basic in any organization where people are working together officially. The pastor who accepts this fact and learns how to work with people, rather than against them, is well on his way to a better, more productive ministry. A sad church situation results when the pastor perceives the decision-making group on the church board as the enemy. The power structure is a sociological fact of life with which pastors and lay leaders must live.

2. *A second important concept in understanding church board behavior is the reference group.* In 1890, William James wrote, "A man has as many social selves as there are distinct groups about which he cares." Reference groups are those groups with which a person identifies, or aspires to identify.

Church board members are always influenced by persons or groups not present in the board meeting. As a young pastor I became greatly confused when I found that a person would talk to me one way over a cup of coffee, man to man, and take a quite different view when the official meeting of the church board was called to order. The fact is that in a man-to-man relationship a person may speak for himself, while in a church board meeting there is always the tendency for people to feel that they are representing groups, imagined or actual. I well remember a wonderful gentleman in our church board who spoke on every issue that ever came up. And he always gave the point of view of the old-timers, although they were not necessarily responsible for his being on the board nor did they look to him for leadership. He made his contribution by telling how things were done 30 years ago.

A training film on reference groups pictured a conference table around which were seated a pastor, superintendent of schools, PTA chairman, bank president, labor leader, and the owner of the lumberyard. With a subject at hand they began to discuss the matter freely. But as each member leaned forward to speak, there was a montage—picture within a picture—on the screen. And without the other members of the group realizing it, each man would look up to see the persons or the groups who were giving their signals to him on how he should respond to the issues at hand. None of the persons seated around the table really spoke for himself. The pastor spoke for his church and his denomination. The banker tended to speak for the moneyed people of the community. The labor leader spoke for all of the blue-collar workers. The PTA chairman represented the mothers. And the owner of the lumberyard represented the business community. Therefore, a pastor who learns how to understand the reference groups represented by the members of his board will understand more fully the responses they give to the various discussion matters at hand.

There are several kinds of reference groups. (1) There is the actual group in session. In each church board there are a few persons whose feelings concern you the most. (2) There is the group each member officially represents, such as the Sunday school, youth group, missionary society, etc. (3) Then there are the abstract groups. These groups cannot be identified accurately. They consist of old-timers, the "spiritual" people, the new people, the poor, the musicians, and others. This reference group affects the board members' responses by its own strong value system. (4) Finally, there is the hangover group. This is a group in the board who have leftover anxieties and problems which have not been relieved. Such a member may react toward the pastor and lay leaders the way he wanted to react toward a person in his office, toward his relatives, or toward the people in his home. Since he was afraid to react toward these people in their respective locations, he will relieve his pent-up feelings in the safer setting of the board.

    3. *The third concept relates to the temperaments of*

people. There are three types of board members in relation to the way they respond to issues at hand:

First, there is the *plunger*. He dives in immediately, is aggressive, and charges through where angels fear to tread. He tests the leadership's permissiveness. He runs up a quick flag to see who salutes it. He gets things off his chest. He is simply compelled from within to speak; he cannot stand silence. He expresses his own feelings freely, but generally before they are thought through.

Then there is the *watcher*. This conservative board member sits back and watches what happens to those who do dive in. He learns how to react to leadership by seeing how leadership handles the plunger. He gets the opinions of others and sees which way things are going. He often sees himself as a mediator. He primarily evaluates the feelings of others and is more interested in their feelings than in his own.

And finally, there is the *well-adjusted* board member who responds spontaneously to the problem at hand. He is neither compulsive nor inhibited. His responses, therefore, are relevant and not lightly dismissed. He reaches his decisions by the orderly process of thinking them through, praying them through, and discussing them through.

4. *The fourth concept on the behavior of board members has to do with the four basic kinds of church board problems.* A board member may be responding with words and feelings to help satisfy one or more needs as follows:

First are the *publicly stated problems*. There is the issue officially before the group. Presumably everyone is addressing his attention to this stated problem. The issue, for instance, may be the challenge of building a new parsonage.

Second are the *hidden problems* not explicitly formulated. The board member may be addressing himself to the problem at hand while he is actually more concerned about another problem which has not been mentioned openly. He may, for instance, really be in favor of building a parsonage but is afraid to vote for it for fear the board may be forced to give the bid to a construction company man who is a member of the church.

Third are the *individual efforts* to achieve ends to which members were committed prior to the meeting. There are times when a member may express restlessness over a problem that does not concern others. He may be determined to bring an issue to the attention of the group or make an exaggerated effort to get some kind of information which does not concern others. This kind of behavior comes because of some commitment made to himself and others prior to the meeting.

And fourth is the individual who must deal with his own hidden problems of *membership anxiety*. In the responses this person makes to issues, he may reveal his own private problems with the group, such as acceptance or his desire to have the group "told off" on certain issues.

5. *The fifth concept concerns motivation.* In every group as large as the church board, there are three kinds of persons always present. There is the *tradition-directed* person, the *inner-directed* person, and the *other-directed* person.

The *tradition-directed person* will always want to keep things like they have been. He will honestly feel more comfortable and possibly even more "spiritual" if the hour of the Sunday night service is kept at the traditional hour rather than be set ahead to a more appropriate time for families with young children. The tradition-directed person finds it very difficult to vote for new programs which are going to break up old constellations of people, places, and things. This person always feels best if things will continue to be done like they have been done.

The *inner-directed person* is highly motivated toward a clear-cut goal. This person has an inner gyroscope. He is directed toward behavior that is consistent, whether he is alone or with others, in the light or in the dark. This is the kind of person for whom folks step aside on the sidewalk. Dr. David Reismann, who first presented this set of insights in *The Lonely Crowd*, says that the inner-directed men are the ones who have made America great. They founded the universities, established the churches, built the railroads, became captains of industry. These are men who have analyzed the future, decided on certain options, and have given every moment of their time and every thrust of their energy toward reaching these goals.

In late years America has developed a new kind of *person who is other-directed*. This kind of individual is much more concerned with what others are doing and thinking than he is with his own set of values and ideals. In the secular world, the other-directed man has a set of morals based on what everybody is doing. If everybody is doing it, then it must be right. This kind of individual on a church board is forever looking across the fence to see what the other denominations are doing. He feels that whatever other churches are doing must be right because perhaps there are more of them than there are of us, or because it has received much publicity.

6. *The sixth concept concerning board behavior relates to cultural determinism.* There was a time when people were born in a community, grew up there, attended school, and lived out their days on a farm or in a business in that same community. But the early American dream of Washington and Jefferson for every man to own his own piece of land where he would support his family has long since dissolved into a nightmare of great cities which contain millions of people who have been brought together from all kinds of backgrounds. Contributing to this melting pot of humanity has been a combination of a world war in which men were transplanted from place to place, and the tendency of modern industry to move men from one city to another as they go up the corporate ladder.

The effective pastors and lay leaders might as well accept the fact that there is a cultural determinism in individual behavior. Every person is the product of all that has ever happened to him and how he related to it. This accounts for some conflicting views on board issues, particularly when the issues fit the convenient niches of "conservative" or "liberal." A young man coming off a sharecroppers' farm in south Mississippi will never be able to understand fully the thinking of a professional man who has been educated in Boston. Nor will a young man who lived in a penthouse on Fifth Avenue in New York ever understand fully the attitudes of a boy who was raised on a Dakota farm. Nor will a teen-ager who grew up near Hollywood and Vine in southern California ever fully understand the values of a person who was raised in a country church in southern Indiana. Everyone comes from his own background with his own set of values and priorities. These are more and more mixed up in membership on church boards as congregations become melting pots of people from various parts of the country.

As the explanations of church board behavior become more clear, the focus of attention centers, then, on an understanding of these basic factors: the power structure, reference groups, personal temperaments, the kinds of problems confronted, the motivations of people, and cultural determinism. Because of all of these factors, there is an axiom which a pastor may well memorize: *If people behave similarly in a board meeting, they probably do so for different reasons.*

This variety of people on a church board makes harmony an all the more remarkable achievement. The apostles of Jesus were a microcosm of many church boards today. Among the apostles was a variety of men who were once known for their impulsiveness, their stubborn, doubting ways, their explosive tempers, and their personal ambition for recognition and place. The only explanation on earth for their unity and commitment which sent them out to work together was the transforming power of the Holy Spirit. This same transforming power will bring church board members together in harmony when they really have every other reason to be at odds.

CHAPTER 6

Organizing the Church Board for Effectiveness

The problems every church board deals with come from four sources.

First, there are the problems which *originate from a higher authority.* Examples of these kinds of problems include civic demands such as meeting building codes and tax payments, mandates, from the denominational headquarters or the district, such as the raising of assessments or budgets.

Second, there are the problems which *come from sudden changes* over which the board has no control. Insurance companies call these happenings "acts of God." These include such things as storms, floods, and falling rocks. The tragedy can be the loss of a person on whom the congregation has leaned, as well as some physical damage to the church or parsonage property.

Third, there are the problems which *originate in needs felt* by one or more members within the board. It may be that the board members are eager for a program of expansion, refurbishing of the sanctuary, increased staff and services to the congregation, or are concerned over personal problems relating to the pastor.

And *fourth* are the *routine problems* which must be expedited on a regular basis. These include the monthly bills, reports, and current planning. It is not likely that a board will want to take time each month to vote to pay the light bill. This is routine.

It does not really matter what the nature of the problems are, or their source. The important issue is how the board will be organized for effectiveness in dealing with all the issues which are brought to its attention. In some cases, one strong person may exercise a virtual veto or endorsement on each item of business. This strong person may be either a layman or the minister. If a layman is boss, the authority tends more to be negative. The strong man may be able to stop programs but not necessarily to initiate them. If this strong person is the pastor, he has assumed a disastrous role. In either case, this is an unproductive way to deal with church board issues.

Another way to deal with church board problems is open discussion. In this type of operation any board member at any time may introduce an idea which in turn is hashed about at great length or quickly dismissed. The discussions in an open discussion session are often characterized by one or more of the following: (1) numerous discussion "excursions"; (2) emphasis on inconsequential aspects of the problem; (3) many side remarks unrelated to the discussion; (4) tendency to discuss unimportant matters at great length and pass big projects without sufficient sharing of ideas.

For many effective congregations, the committee system has been adopted as the most effective way for organizing people productively. With the church board divided into working committees, all items of business are immediately referred to proper committees. The following observations may be made concerning such board structure:

1. Each committee has at least one meeting between board sessions. These meetings may or may not be attended

by the pastor. But at these sessions the committee may originate business or deal with business which has been referred to it by the board.

2. Each committee, between board sessions, implements previous legislation which refers to its area of responsibility. This means that the church board does not act as a jury voting thumbs-up or thumbs-down on the programs presented to them by the pastor. The board votes to legislate work for themselves to do. This method of organizing people's energy multiplies, many times over, the energies of the pastor.

3. Each committee reports at the regular monthly meeting of the board. As the committee system becomes more accepted by the board, these committee reports are expedited quickly. Confidence increases as members begin to see the thoroughness with which each committee has done its work.

4. After the church board has become adjusted to the committee system, there is a growing tendency to refer business to a committee with power to act. This not only builds great confidences, but cuts down on the length of board meetings.

5. In the committee system the pastor serves in the role of "chairman of the board." His leadership in ideas and direction is exerted primarily through committees and committee chairmen. He is not "on the spot" in every board meeting to make decisions and to come up with solutions to every problem the church faces.

There are certain advantages to the committee system. (1) More study is given to each problem. (2) It releases the potential of each person to serve. (3) The pastor is taken off the spot about "his" ideas. (4) Committees tend to develop respect for each other's work. (5) A number of people have a detailed knowledge of each problem or idea reported to the board.

However, there are also certain disadvantages in the committee system which must be faced: (1) The process of spreading responsibility and involvement is a slower process than a dictatorship. (2) Things can die in committee without action being taken. Ways must be devised for keeping issues alive. This may be done by a new referral in the next board meeting with a reference to the fact that it is another referral.

The committee system necessitates good communications. It is best to mimeograph church board minutes and to mail them to all members immediately after each meeting, so committee people can know what their work assignments are.

Suggested Church Board Committees and Their Responsibilities

A. *Program and Planning Committee*
  1. Revivals and evangelism
  2. Operation of church office
  3. Visitation program
  4. Kitchen
  5. Church social life
  6. Church calendar
  7. Advertising
  8. Music
  9. Communion preparation

B. *Finance Committee*
  1. Budgeting
  2. Accounting and banking procedures
  3. Budget control
  4. Supervision of purchasing
  5. Increase of church stewardship
  6. Tax records

C. *Christian Education Committee*
1. Operation of the Sunday school
2. Children's church
3. Vacation Bible school
4. Wednesday night children's meetings
5. Sunday night children's meetings

D. *Buildings and Grounds Committee*
1. Cleaning of the church
2. Maintenance and repair of church and parsonage
3. Refurbishing, remodeling, and expansion of buildings
4. Church parking
5. Church equipment, including musical instruments
6. Parsonage equipment

E. *Pastor and Parish Committee*
Advises with the pastor on personal matters within the church family

F. *Building Committee*
Named only when a building project is at hand

There are several ways to appoint committees. One is to ask the pastor to appoint the chairmen and the board members suggest their own preferences on committee membership assignment. The exception would be the Pastor and Parish Committee, which is made up of the chairmen of the first four committees with the pastor.

It is not necessary for the pastor to meet with each committee each time it is called. In fact, the committees will tend to do better work if they are cut free and are not dominated by the pastor. This does not mean the pastor has a lack of interest. Nor does it mean he is not aware of what is happening. His close relationship to the chairman of the committee and other committee members will assure him of full information. But it does mean that he will let the committee do its own work.

Committee meetings may be scheduled at any time. Sometimes during a regular board meeting, time can be given for committee work. The following suggested agenda makes provision for just such an arrangement.

> Call to order
> Opening devotions
> Reading of the minutes
> Mimeographed report from the pastor
> Mimeographed report from the treasurer
> Matters of reference
> Committee meetings
> Committee reports
> Adjournment

The biggest single hurdle to implementing the church board committee system is the unwillingness of pastors to release authority to laymen. But once laymen are convinced that the pastor means business in allowing them to use their judgment and their energies in carrying on the secular side of the church assignment, it is amazing how they will grow and develop into strong leaders. Furthermore, this intensity of interest will carry over into the spiritual aspects of the church's program.

MAKING SUNDAY AN EVENT

CHAPTER 7

A Morning Service
That Inspires

William Barclay said that the preacher must try to give his people three things every Sunday morning.[1] First, he must give them *something to feel*. He says plainly that "no great preacher was ever afraid of emotion." Everything that happens in the morning service must give the impression that it all matters intensely. Music, sermon, prayer, Bible reading, and offering must be possessed of feeling. If what is happening doesn't matter to the preacher, the singers, organist, pianist, and ushers, it probably won't matter to anyone else either.

Second, Dr. Barclay said that the morning service must give the people *something to think about*. It is not enough to feel the emotion of the moment. There must be something to remember and think about when the service is over. A nebulous, golden haze of emotion is not long-lasting. It is not enough to remember how you felt in a service. It is also necessary to take away from church something to think on and talk about all week. A new spiritual insight, a story, or an idea must come alive. As a thought is turned over in the mind and talked about in the marketplace, where truth is practiced, it becomes indelibly submerged in the mind, never to be fully forgotten. This gives the service a lasting, even an eternal quality.

And finally, Dr. Barclay said,

> Even if the preacher provides something to feel and something to remember, he has not completed his task. He must finally provide something to do. Every service must be a challenge to action, in regard to one's self, or in regard to others, or both. It is a psychological fact that the oftener an emotion is stirred without accompanying action, the less likely it is that action will ever happen. It becomes in the end very easy to make emotion a substitute for action.[2]

If the inner man, or soul, consists of mind, emotions, and will, then Dr. Barclay has made his appeal for the Sunday morning service to meet the whole person. The parking-lot facilities, form-fitting pews, correct heat, and all other preparations are designed for one purpose, to make the inner man as susceptible as possible to having his emotions moved, his mind stirred, and his will activated. For this purpose the sanctuary should be the Sunday morning headquarters for Inspiration Incorporated.

However, for many people in many churches, the morning service is a mild depressant in which the mind and emotions receive a mild, negative scolding with different variations on the theme, "You ought to be and do something you aren't and don't." The only place the will enters into the picture is on the way out, when a firm resolution is made not to come back.

Bishop Gerald Kennedy in his book, *For Laymen and Other Martyrs*, describes his personal disappointment and depression in attending some churches:

> Sometimes when I am in church, the service gets off on such a low note that I never recover my confidence. You know how it is. Starts are so important that a bad one kills a fellow's expectancy.
>
> The kind of thing I am referring to usually has a call to worship in a subdued mood, as if it were time for bed and mother is calming her child with a lullaby. It is often

"good" music and like as not somebody such as Beethoven or Brahms wrote it. The music experts, of which I am not one, think it is great and close their eyes in bliss.

Then the choir starts down the aisle to the opening hymn. The hymn chosen would be excellent for a wake, and the choir members stroll along as if they were members of the bereaved family. They do not march; they meander. By this time I am getting drowsy and it is hard to cover up the yawns.

The minister gets into the spirit of the thing and gives forth with an invocation that is gentle and no more invigorating than the hum of bees in summer. Everything is so well-mannered and genteel that I hope they never find out what I am thinking.[3]

But, thank God, not all the churches are losers. Churches that are filled on Sunday morning meet needs people feel. After six days at hard labor, people are ready to be inspired, helped, cured, guided. Churches that are full have become way stations for people who anticipate help for themselves and their families. Dr. Kennedy describes these services in glowing terms:

But once in a while I am in a service that is quite different and wonderful. The call to worship sounds like trumpets, not violins. One I remember with joy gave us the opening line of "A Mighty Fortress Is Our God." Great! The processional hymn was four/four time and full of affirmations about God's majesty and power. The choir members marched as if they were going somewhere and they did not have all day to get there. Wonderful!

The preacher reminded us who we were and what we were gathered together to proclaim. He spoke strongly of the greatness of our God and the majesty of the Church of Christ. I tell you I could hardly wait for the next thing to happen, and drowsing or yawning was so far from me that I was invigorated and felt like saying Hallelujah.

Now this is the way a Christian service of worship ought to start and continue, for this is the way of the Christian faith. We are not called by our Lord to rest and retreat but to joy and life. We do not gather in the church to drone through prayers and hymns but to hear a bugle. Our mood should be that of a baseball or football crowd's when the trumpet rings out and they yell "Charge!" For weariness is not cured by boredom but by inspiration.[4]

But how can the pastor of a small church make his sanctuary the headquarters for inspiration and help?

The first step is to decide in advance what the service is to achieve. As any good homiletics student knows, the beginning of any good sermon is to write down in one short sentence at the top of the page what the sermon is to achieve. And the beginning of the preparation for an inspiring Sunday morning service is to write down the primary purpose of the service. Although the Holy Spirit will apply the blessings of a good service to as many needs as there are people present, the blessings seem to pour more freely in a service with a central theme or purpose. Here are some themes or statements of purpose to which many hearts will respond on almost any Sunday morning:

1. Exalt the cross of Christ.

2. Bring people to a decision to confess their sins and accept Christ as Lord and Master of their lives.

3. Inspire believers to take the step of faith toward a wholly sanctified life.

4. Encourage people who have had a tough week.

5. Demonstrate the love of Christ for young people.

6. Apply the great teachings of the Apostle Paul to the problems of Christians in families.

7. Inspire people to self-denial for the Thanksgiving Offering.

8. Impress people anew with the love of Christ.

9. Help people appreciate more the living Church of Jesus Christ.

10. Make prayer meaningful to everyone in church.

11. Challenge the people to participate in fasting.

12. Make the Bible come alive as the living Word of God.

13. Challenge the people to a program of Christian action in our community.

Several things need to be noted about these objectives:

1. Since human need is of infinite variety and the Bible is of unfathomed depth, there is no end to the specific needs of human beings which may be met in an inspired morning worship service which gets its authority from God's Word.

2. Once the theme of the service is clearly defined, then everything else tends to fall into place. The hymns relate to the theme, hopefully. The scripture reading has direct purpose. The morning prayer has direction, and the special music becomes a ministry and not a performance.

3. This kind of advance planning requires long-range goals. The general direction may well be chosen roughly as follows:

September: Themes of challenge relating to the church locally and generally

October and November: Themes relating to home and family with a concluding service on Thanksgiving Sunday

December: Themes on Christ and Christmas

January to Lent: Themes on personal Christian growth and development

Beginning of Lent to Easter: Themes on Christ and the Cross

Easter to Pentecost: Themes on the Holy Spirit and sanctification

June: Themes on young people and their needs as suggested by graduation, weddings, and the end of another school year

July and August: Repeat the themes which have been of special blessing, using the sermon series title "Sermons You Asked For."

September: Start a new cycle.

4. This approach need not interfere with systematic expository preaching. The theme of the service can be chosen on the basis of the sermon theme.

5. This system takes discipline. There is little or no place for reminiscing in between songs unless the flights back into time enhance the purpose of the service.

6. Announcements are another problem. It has been solved in many churches by placing the announcements before the service or after the benediction.

A score card was kept privately by a TV station manager in my congregation. It may or may not be helpful to other pastors. It looked like this:

THEME: EXALTING THE CROSS OF CHRIST	A	B	C	D	E	F
Prelude						
Call to Worship						
Opening Hymn						
Scripture Reading						
Choir Number						
Morning Prayer						
Offering						
Solo						
Sermon						
Closing Hymn						
Announcements						
Benediction						
Postlude						

Besides the theme which is rooted in human need and the Word of God, the service of inspiration needs the authority of the Bible in more than a casual reading of a lesson prior to the service. Here is one kind of bulletin format which makes great use of the Scriptures:

MORNING WORSHIP

ENTER TO WORSHIP: "Unto him be glory in the church by Christ Jesus throughout all ages, world without end. Amen" (Eph. 3:21).

Call to worship by the choir
Invocation by the pastor

HYMN: "Crown Him with Many Crowns"   No. 458

SCRIPTURE: Psalms 23   This psalm tells in poetic simplicity the marvelous relationship there is between Christ, the Good Shepherd, and the believers, who are His followers.

CHOIR: "The King of Love My Shepherd Is"

WORSHIP THROUGH PRAYER: "And ye shall seek me, and find me, when ye shall search for me with all your heart" (Jer. 29:13).

WORSHIP THROUGH GIVING: "Honour the Lord with thy substance, and with the firstfruits of all thine increase" (Prov. 3:9).

SOLO: Mr. Paul Jensen

SERMON: "The Therapy of God: Psalms 23"

MIXED QUARTET:
"Saviour, like a Shepherd Lead Us"

BENEDICTION

DOXOLOGY

Even if the Bible passages are not read before each part of the service, their presence in the bulletin is its own testimony.

A Source Book

The following materials may be useful in developing Sunday morning services of inspiration and power.

> *Call to Worship*

1. *For where two or three are gathered together in my name, there am I in the midst of them* (Matt. 18:20).

2. *As his custom was, he went into the synagogue on the sabbath day, and stood up for to read* (Luke 4:16).

3. *Unto him be glory in the church by Christ Jesus throughout all ages, world without end. Amen* (Eph. 3:21).

4. *Christ also loved the church, and gave himself for it; that he might present it to himself a glorious church* (Eph. 5:25, 27).

5. *Let the word of Christ dwell in you richly in all wisdom; teaching and admonishing one another in psalms and hymns and spiritual songs, singing with grace in your hearts to the Lord* (Col. 3:16).

6. *He that hath an ear, let him hear what the Spirit saith unto the churches; To him that overcometh will I give to eat of the tree of life, which is in the midst of the paradise of God* (Rev. 2:7).

7. *That at the name of Jesus every knee should bow, of things in heaven, and things in earth, and things under the earth* (Phil. 2:10).

8. *Surely the Lord is in this place* (Gen. 28:16).

9. *He that dwelleth in the secret place of the most High shall abide under the shadow of the Almighty* (Ps. 91:1).

10. *Strength and beauty are in his sanctuary* (Ps. 96:6).

11. *Take my yoke upon you, and learn of me; for I am*

meek and lowly in heart: and ye shall find rest unto your souls (Matt. 11:29).

12. *All scripture is given by inspiration of God, and is profitable for doctrine, for reproof, for correction, for instruction in righteousness* (II Tim. 3:16).

13. *Receive with meekness the engrafted word, which is able to save your souls* (Jas. 1:21).

14. *We then that are strong ought to bear the infirmities of the weak, and not to please ourselves* (Rom. 15:1).

15. *Mine house shall be called an house of prayer for all people* (Isa. 56:7).

16. *They found him in the temple, sitting in the midst of the doctors, both hearing them, and asking them questions* (Luke 2:46).

17. *They shall speak of the glory of thy kingdom, and talk of thy power* (Ps. 145:11).

18. *By him therefore let us offer the sacrifice of praise to God continually, that is, the fruit of our lips giving thanks to his name* (Heb. 13:15).

19. *We cannot but speak the things which we have seen and heard* (Acts 4:20).

20. *He reasoned of righteousness, temperance, and judgment to come* (Acts 24:25).

21. *We took sweet counsel together, and walked unto the house of God in company* (Ps. 55:14).

22. *God is a Spirit: and they that worship him must worship him in spirit and in truth* (John 4:24).

23. *Speaking to yourselves in psalms and hymns and spiritual songs, singing and making melody in your heart to the Lord* (Eph. 5:19).

24. *Present your bodies a living sacrifice, holy, acceptable unto God, which is your reasonable service* (Rom. 12:1).

25. *Thou wilt shew me the path of life: in thy presence is fulness of joy; at thy right hand there are pleasures for evermore* (Ps. 16:11).

26. *I bring you good tidings of great joy, which shall be to all people* (Luke 2:10).

27. *Let us be glad and rejoice, and give honour to him: for the marriage of the Lamb is come, and his wife hath made herself ready* (Rev. 19:7).

28. *Glorify God in your body, and in your spirit, which are God's* (I Cor. 6:20).

29. *Wait on the Lord; be of good courage, and he shall strengthen thine heart: wait, I say, on the Lord* (Ps. 27:14).

30. *O come, let us worship and bow down: let us kneel before the Lord our maker* (Ps. 95:6).

31. *Blessing, and honour, and glory, and power, be unto him that sitteth upon the throne, and unto the Lamb for ever and ever* (Rev. 5:13).

> ## Morning Hymns

1. "A Charge to Keep I Have"
2. "A Mighty Fortress Is Our God"
3. "All Hail the Power of Jesus' Name"
4. "Arise, My Soul, Arise"
5. "Beneath the Cross of Jesus"
6. "Blessed Assurance"
7. "Come, Thou Almighty King"
8. "Come, Thou Fount"
9. "Crown Him with Many Crowns"
10. "Fairest Lord Jesus"
11. "Faith of Our Fathers"
12. "For the Beauty of the Earth"
13. "From Every Stormy Wind"
14. "Guide Me, O Thou Great Jehovah"
15. "He Leadeth Me"
16. "Holy Ghost, with Light Divine"
17. "Holy, Holy, Holy"
18. "How Firm a Foundation"
19. "I Love Thy Kingdom, Lord"
20. "In Heavenly Love Abiding"

21. "Jesus, Lover of My Soul"
22. "Lead On, O King Eternal"
23. "Love Divine"
24. "Majestic Sweetness"
25. "Meditation"
26. "More Love to Thee"
27. "My Faith Looks Up to Thee"
28. "Oh, for a Heart to Praise My God"
29. "Oh, for a Thousand Tongues to Sing"
30. "O God, Our Help in Ages Past"
31. "O Sacred Head, Now Wounded"
32. "Oh, Worship the King"
33. "O Zion, Haste"
34. "Praise Him, Praise Him"
35. "Take Time to Be Holy"
36. "The Church's One Foundation"
37. "Trust and Obey"
38. "When I Survey"

▶ *Prayer Verses*

1. *The prayer of the upright is his delight* (Prov. 15:8).

2. *He went out, and departed into a solitary place, and there prayed* (Mark 1:35).

3. *Continuing instant in prayer* (Rom. 12:12).

4. *I will therefore that men pray every where, lifting up holy hands, without wrath and doubting* (I Tim. 2:8).

5. *Seek the Lord and his strength, seek his face continually* (I Chron. 16:11).

6. *Mine eye mourneth by reason of affliction: Lord, I have called daily upon thee, I have stretched out my hands unto thee* (Ps. 88:9).

7. *Daniel kneeled upon his knees three times a day, and prayed, and gave thanks before his God* (Dan. 6:10).

8. *And when thou prayest, thou shalt not be as the hypocrites are: for they love to pray standing in the syna-*

gogues and in the corners of the streets, that they may be seen of men. Verily I say unto you, They have their reward (Matt. 6:5).

9. *But when ye pray, use not vain repetitions, as the heathen do; for they think that they shall be heard for their much speaking* (Matt. 6:7).

10. *For where two or three are gathered together in my name, there am I in the midst of them* (Matt. 18:20).

11. *Watch and pray, that ye enter not into temptation: the spirit indeed is willing, but the flesh is weak* (Matt. 26:41).

12. *And he said unto them, This kind can come forth by nothing, but by prayer and fasting* (Mark 9:29).

13. *And as he prayed, the fashion of his countenance was altered, and his raiment was white and glistering* (Luke 9:29).

14. *And he spake a parable unto them to this end, that men ought always to pray, and not to faint* (Luke 18:1).

15. *And when they had prayed, the place was shaken where they were assembled together; and they were all filled with the Holy Ghost, and they spake the word of God with boldness* (Acts 4:31).

16. *I will pray with the spirit, and I will pray with the understanding also: I will sing with the spirit, and I will sing with the understanding also* (I Cor. 14:15).

17. *For this child I prayed; and the Lord hath given me my petition which I asked of him* (I Sam. 1:27).

18. *Therefore thou deliveredst them into the hand of their enemies, who vexed them: and in the time of their trouble, when they cried unto thee, thou heardest them from heaven; and according to thy manifold mercies thou gavest them saviours, who saved them out of the hand of their enemies* (Neh. 9:27).

19. *The Lord is far from the wicked; but he heareth the prayer of the righteous* (Prov. 15:29).

20. *And ye shall seek me, and find me, when ye shall search for me with all your heart* (Jer. 29:13).

21. *Ask, and it shall be given you; seek, and ye shall find; knock, and it shall be opened unto you* (Matt. 7:7).

22. *If two of you shall agree on earth as touching any thing that they shall ask, it shall be done for them of my Father which is in heaven* (Matt. 18:19).

23. *Therefore I say unto you, What things soever ye desire, when ye pray, believe that ye receive them, and ye shall have them* (Mark 11:24).

24. *If ye abide in me, and my words abide in you, ye shall ask what ye will, and it shall be done unto you* (John 15:7).

25. *Ye ask, and receive not, because ye ask amiss, that ye may consume it upon your lusts* (Jas. 4:3).

26. *And the prayer of faith shall save the sick, and the Lord shall raise him up; and if he have committed sins, they shall be forgiven him* (Jas. 5:15).

27. *Confess your faults one to another, and pray one for another, that ye may be healed* (Jas. 5:16).

➤ *Offering Verses*

1. *Remember the words of the Lord Jesus, how he said, It is more blessed to give than to receive* (Acts 20:35).

2. *And when they had opened their treasures, they presented unto him gifts; gold, and frankincense, and myrrh* (Matt. 2:11).

3. *As every man hath received the gift, even so minister the same one to another, as good stewards of the manifold grace of God* (I Pet. 4:10).

4. *Every man shall give as he is able, according to the blessing of the Lord thy God which he hath given thee* (Deut. 16:17).

5. *For all things come of thee, and of thine own have we given thee* (I Chron. 29:14).

6. *Cast thy bread upon the waters: for thou shalt find it after many days* (Eccles. 11:1).

7. *But rather give alms of such things as ye have; and, behold, all things are clean unto you* (Luke 11:41).

8. *For all these have of their abundance cast in unto the offerings of God: but she of her penury hath cast in all the living that she had* (Luke 21:4).

9. *Every man according as he purposeth in his heart, so let him give; not grudgingly, or of necessity: for God loveth a cheerful giver* (II Cor. 9:7).

10. *For ye know the grace of our Lord Jesus Christ, that, though he was rich, yet for your sakes he became poor, that ye through his poverty might be rich* (II Cor. 8:9).

11. *Look not every man on his own things, but every man also on the things of others* (Phil. 2:4).

12. *Honour the Lord with thy substance, and with the firstfruits of all thine increase* (Prov. 3:9).

13. *This poor widow hath cast more in, than all they which have cast into the treasury* (Mark 12:43).

14. *Thy prayers and thine alms are come up for a memorial before God* (Acts 10:4).

15. *Surely goodness and mercy shall follow me all the days of my life: and I will dwell in the house of the Lord for ever* (Ps. 23:6).

16. *Blessed be the Lord: for he hath shewed me his marvellous kindness in a strong city* (Ps. 31:21).

17. *The liberal soul shall be made fat: and he that watereth shall be watered also himself* (Prov. 11:25).

18. *He which soweth sparingly shall reap also sparingly; and he which soweth bountifully shall reap also bountifully* (II Cor. 9:6).

19. *Give, and it shall be given unto you; good measure, pressed down, and shaken together, and running over* (Luke 6:38).

20. *But by an equality, that now at this time your abundance may be a supply for their want* (II Cor. 8:14).

❯ Closing Hymns

1. "A Charge to Keep I Have"
2. "All for Jesus"
3. "All That Thrills My Soul"
4. "All to Jesus I Surrender"
5. "At Calvary"
6. "At the Cross"
7. "Beneath the Cross of Jesus"
8. "Break Thou the Bread of Life"
9. "Close to Thee"
10. "Fill Me Now"
11. "For You I Am Praying"
12. "Give of Your Best to the Master"
13. "God Leads Us Along"
14. "Hallelujah, What a Saviour"
15. "Have Thine Own Way, Lord"
16. "He Hideth My Soul"
17. "Hiding in Thee"
18. "His Yoke Is Easy"
19. "I Am Coming, Lord"
20. "I Gave My Life for Thee"
21. "I Know I Love Thee Better, Lord"
22. "I Need Thee Every Hour"
23. "I Will Praise Him"
24. "I'll Live for Him"
25. "Jesus Is All I Need"
26. "Jesus Is Mine"
27. "Jesus, Lover of My Soul"
28. "Jesus Will Walk with Me"
29. "Lead Me to Calvary"
30. "Living for Jesus"
31. "More Love to Thee"
32. "Must Jesus Bear the Cross?"

33. "Near the Cross"
34. "Near to the Heart of God"
35. "Only Trust Him"
36. "Rock of Ages"
37. "Saviour, like a Shepherd Lead Us"
38. "Sweet Hour of Prayer"
39. "Take My Life and Let It Be"
40. "Take Time to Be Holy"
41. "The Beautiful Garden of Prayer"
42. "The Closer I Walk"
43. "The Great Physician"
44. "The Haven of Rest"
45. "The Old Rugged Cross"
46. "Whiter than Snow"
47. "Yield Not to Temptation"

> *Benedictions*

1. *Unto him that loved us, and washed us from our sins in his own blood, and hath made us kings and priests unto God and his Father; to him be glory and dominion for ever and ever. Amen* (Rev. 1:5-6).

2. *Now unto him that is able to keep you from falling, and to present you faultless before the presence of his glory with exceeding joy, to the only wise God our Saviour, be glory and majesty, dominion and power, both now and ever. Amen* (Jude 24-25).

3. *Now the God of peace, that brought again from the dead our Lord Jesus, that great shepherd of the sheep, through the blood of the everlasting covenant, make you perfect in every good work to do his will, working in you that which is well pleasing in his sight, through Jesus Christ; to whom be glory for ever and ever. Amen* (Heb. 13:20-21).

4. *Now unto the King eternal, immortal, invisible, the only wise God, be honour and glory for ever and ever. Amen* (I Tim. 1:17).

5. *And the Lord make you to increase and abound in love one toward another, and toward all men, even as we do toward you; to the end he may stablish your hearts unblameable in holiness before God, even our Father, at the coming of our Lord Jesus Christ with all his saints* (I Thess. 3:12-13).

6. *Now unto him that is able to do exceeding abundantly above all that we ask or think, according to the power that worketh in us, unto him be glory in the church by Christ Jesus throughout all ages, world without end. Amen* (Eph. 3:20-21).

7. *The grace of the Lord Jesus Christ, and the love of God, and the communion of the Holy Ghost, be with you all. Amen* (II Cor. 13:14).

8. *The Lord bless thee, and keep thee. The Lord make his face to shine upon thee, and be gracious unto thee: the Lord lift up his countenance upon thee, and give thee peace* (Num. 6:24-26).

CHAPTER 8

A Night Service That Brings Them Back

The pastor of a large city church reported to his Monday morning golfing partners: "I pastor one of those churches that is not quite full in the morning and not quite empty at night."

A new pastor was told by a board member on his first Sunday morning: "Now, our people do pretty well in the morning, but at night you could fire a shotgun across this church with little fear of hitting anyone."

One pastor who bragged about his three Sunday morning services was challenged to start a Sunday night service. His response was, "I'll leave the Sunday night service to you evangelicals. I've never had the nerve."

He had no nerve to start a Sunday night service for some obvious reasons: (1) Many families plan to confine their churchgoing to once a week—on Sunday morning. (2) As more and more people live in suburban areas, commuting to church in the city on Sunday night seems to many to be too much of a chore. (3) The pressures of living take their toll in weekend exhaustion, real or imagined. (4) Sunday school, morning service, Sunday family dinner, youth meeting, and night service have made Sunday for many people not much of a day of rest. It is for many the most exhausting day of the week.

But, beyond these problems, there are two basic reasons why Sunday night attendances usually are low in many churches. First, there is every evidence that the pastor considers the night service to be of considerably less priority than the morning service. Space given in the Sunday bulletin to the night service is often a small fraction of the space given to the morning service. The very content and delivery of the night sermon indicates it has a second place in the pastor's preparation for Sunday. The deportment of the choir and ushers, even the way they dress, often indicates their feelings of lower importance for the night service. And what tries to pass for informality on the platform is often obvious to the congregation as unpreparedness. Poor sermon preparation and lack of prepared music cannot be hid for long behind prolonged attempts to cover up with "testimony time." Testimonies are far too important to be used as a shield to hide unpreparedness. If a Sunday night service is going to be a useful tool in transforming the small church, everything about it must indicate the pastor and the church board believe the night service to be of utmost importance—a full equal to the morning service.

The second basic problem causing low Sunday night attendances is the fact that these services do not meet very many needs people feel. People put forth effort to drive great distances to attend functions which satisfy some personal needs. But in many churches the Sunday night service must depend heavily for attendance on families whose consciences and church attendance habits make them feel guilty when absent. The motivation for attendance actually may be negative instead of positive. If this motivation can be changed to make children, young people, parents, single adults, and the elderly feel they cannot afford to miss the night service, then the church has turned a corner into a new era of growth and development.

Here are some suggestions for transforming the Sunday night service from a second-class duty to a first-class spiritual experience:

1. Lay out the plans for the Sunday night services at least four weeks in advance, including music, special features, and sermon.

2. Begin announcing what will be happening in these Sunday night services in advance as though they were events and not routine schedule.

3. Give equal space in the bulletin for both the Sunday morning and Sunday night services.

4. In the midweek mailer give more space to the music, special features, and sermon in the Sunday night service than is given to either the morning service or Sunday school.

5. In the church-page advertisement on Saturday, feature the night service regularly. If the night service grows, the morning attendance will carry itself.

6. As a matter of discipline, complete the weekly preparations for the night service before turning full attention to the morning service. Prepare the night sermon before writing the morning message.

7. Examine the time of the night service. Needs vary among congregations, but for most people the later hour on Sunday night is a hangover from an earlier agrarian time schedule which was built around farm-chore times. Sunday night is a school night in that children have to attend classes

the next day. And people have to go to work on Monday morning, sometimes very early. One church increased its Sunday night attendance by nearly 50 percent by moving the service time one hour earlier.

8. Provide full and competent nursery facilities and supervision for Sunday nights. It is more important then than on Sunday morning.

9. Night services often close with an evangelistic appeal, but if no one comes forward, do not allow the service to close on a depressing note. The evening has not been wasted because no one came to the altar. The altar is important, but the Lord works in many ways to perform His purposes. Let the service be finally closed, without fail, on a happy, optimistic note.

Although every church will have its own methods, here are some ingredients which have proved helpful in transforming a night service into an event which brings back the people.

1. Choose a good, loud, resounding chorus as a theme to open the service. "Make Me a Blessing" is hard to beat. For years Billy Graham has used "This Is My Story." Sing it through more than once if a repeat helps to lift the spirits of the people. Get them on their feet. And get them smiling. A handshake or a united "Amen" or "Hallelujah" isn't bad if not overdone. But with this opening chorus, let it be known by everyone that the service is under way, on time, and "alive unto God."

2. With the people still standing, let the opening prayer be made without introduction. It is hoped this prayer will be radiant, God-oriented, and short.

3. With the people still on their feet, let the pastor introduce the first of three "Hymns We Love." This first hymn should be the biggest sound of the evening. Choose a song, preferably in four/four time, well-known, and loved. I'm

not sure I can defend this next suggestion, but I always asked the pianist instead of the organist to play the introductions to congregational hymns (even Sunday mornings). The sound of the piano is brighter, crisper, and less likely to be listened to as a substitute for singing. Strive for the type of song and sound often associated with revival, crusade, rally, or camp meeting singing at its best. The second and third songs on Sunday night may be more devotional, and with the people seated. I'm not sure why, but sing all the verses.

4. As I organize the Sunday night service, I always think in blocks of activity that go together. The opening block consists of the theme chorus, invocation, and "Hymns We Love." With all the instruments, choir, pastor, and people, this is the time to project Christian radiance and deep, Spirit-filled joy. If this part of the service fills its role, the rest of the meeting comes much easier. But a dull opening is hard to overcome.

5. The second block of activity is devotional, consisting of two parts, Bible reading and prayer. There can be great variety. For years I have had this scripture reading given by laymen. These were chosen in advance and given written instructions on reading slowly, projecting their voices, and by all means, practicing the passage aloud in advance. They also were given guidance on dress, and were asked to sit on the very front seat or on the platform.

Sunday evening prayers were often made by local laymen or by visiting clergymen and laymen of distinction. Very often three teen-agers, board members, Sunday school teachers, or other groups of common distinction were asked to pray. If I felt moved, I often closed the prayer myself.

6. Unannounced, the prayers were followed by the "Musical Package." This always consisted of three numbers, one leading into the other unannounced. A solo, ensemble,

and choir number were used, singing gospel music, not anthems.

Parenthetically let us consider the "special music" problem. It has been said that a small church does not have adequate talent. I've pastored those small churches and I know how hard music can be to come by. But it can be done. Here are some suggestions:

(a) Soloists are easiest to find. Encourage them to memorize their words and make arrangements for practice in advance. Insist on their sitting near the piano and being ready without awkward loss of time. If microphones are to be used, be sure they are turned on and adjusted in advance.

(b) Children often make excellent Sunday evening singers, either as soloists or in groups.

(c) Most high schools are training instrumentalists as well as singers. As Ron Lush says, "Use them or lose them." Enjoy the sour notes and be glad you've got the young people in church.

(d) Duet teams and trios usually are not hard to recruit. A great variety of books is available for these groups to use.

(e) One of the most often ignored groups is the easiest to recruit—the mixed quartet. They don't need special music. They can sing directly out of the hymnbook. And if you have no choir, the mixed quartet can become the beginning segment of one. Add to it a second foursome and the result is a strong gospel sound to be enjoyed wherever gospel music is sung.

(f) Do not hesitate to recruit special help on a one-time basis from larger churches. These larger churches have more talent than they can use, and such visits to small churches can be a source of blessing to both the musicians and the churches they visit. But check with the pastor. You'll need his cooperation if you ever do it more than once.

(*g*) The only other source of help for the musically deprived church is the miracle of recording. With a little advanced planning and imagination, your church can have the best voices in the business. Even short musical films are now available.

7. The offering always followed the "Musical Package." Since our church operated on a strict monthly budget which was met each and every month, the offering on Sunday night was no casual, unannounced affair. It was important. It was announced. And it was set into the night service at the point when the people might be more likely blessed, more likely feeling rewarded for coming, and thus more likely to give.

8. After the offering came the announcements and special feature. Sometimes the announcements were the special feature. As an aid to making this part of the service different from the rest, the pastor came down from behind the pulpit to the level of the people. A hand mike was used but would not be necessary in a small sanctuary. Some of the special features were as follows:

(*a*) Several people related to key announcements were invited forward. They might be called on to make a one-minute speech, report, or announcement. At other times the pastor used them for reference and made the announcements himself.

(*b*) The interview technique was used many times. Typical persons to be interviewed briefly might be a visiting soldier, teen athlete, a child, Sunday school superintendent, youth or missionary president, a guest of distinction, someone moving away, someone just arrived, graduating seniors, businessmen, and professional people. Really, with a little imagination there is no end to the lineup of persons who may be interviewed to the glory of God. A little practice teaches the interviewer how to ask leading questions which cannot be answered with yes or no and must be amplified.

(c) A favorite among many people was "The Congregational Special." Many people would enjoy singing some of the great church music which is usually reserved for people with trained voices. But they never get to except in the bathtub or riding alone in the car. If the sheet music is secured in advance and the words are clearly printed on a flip chart, the "Congregational Special" becomes a great blessing to the people. Some of the numbers which can be used for this are: "The Holy City," "The Lord's Prayer," "It Took a Miracle," "How Great Thou Art."

A more sophisticated means to enhance the "Congregational Special" is to use the wall of the church as a screen and, along with the words to the music, project onto the same screen appropriate colored slides. If the words are reversed (that is, white letters on a black background), the letters will stand out on the slides so a very striking effect is produced. If this cannot be worked out, project words and pictures side by side.

(d) Another special feature at appropriate times of the year would be simple skits to promote Sunday school attendance, Alabaster giving, district camps and institutes, and patriotic themes.

9. The final block of planning for the night service included a single verse of "Pass Me Not, O Gentle Saviour," the sermon, and the invitation. The sermon had three requirements in its preparation: (1) It must speak to the needs of the people; (2) The content must be interesting; (3) It must be Bible-oriented. To this my three sons added one more requirement—brevity.

To all of the above ideas on a Sunday night service that will bring people back may be added these few miscellaneous suggestions:

1. Do not allow anyone to sing or play who has not practiced in advance with the accompanist to be used during the service.

2. On warm summer evenings it is easier than ever to let down and allow the night services to be a secondary Sunday event. If the choir wear robes in the morning, insist that they do the same at night. Coats and ties for ushers are just as important at night in the summer as they are in the morning. It is not easy to keep the morale high for the Sunday night service through all seasons of the year.

3. At various seasons of the year plan special Sunday night events. These might include:

Gospel song fests
The wedding vows in June
Four Sunday nights of Christmas
Candlelight Communion on Easter Sunday night
Youth services
Special guest speaker
Missionary festival

CHAPTER 9

How to Double
Your Attendance

With the arrival of every new pastor, the congregation and the new man enter upon a honeymoon period characterized by strong intention on the part of preacher and people to make the very most of the new relationship. Hope rises. Superficial improvements and adjustments are made. Familiar sermonic material is preached with fervor. Even the offerings increase.

But, after a while, something happens. The honeymoon comes to a grinding halt. The foundations that were rising to support the new superstructure of church growth begin to crumble, crack, and settle into the bog of dismal statistics. Explanations are dusted off and used again on why church growth at this time is hard or even impossible. The broom that swept clean is now in disarray, the edges frayed, and the beautiful promise of a full sweep has become the same old drag. Is this necessary? No! Churches do grow if they are alive. For it is the nature of anything alive to grow.

Phenomenal statistics can be overwhelming and discouraging, yet they serve a point. Here are some examples: The Garden Grove Church in Orange County, Calif., went from no members to 5,000 in 15 years. The Skyline Wesleyan Church in San Diego grew from nothing to three Sunday schools, three morning services, and two night services in 13 years. Average Sunday school attendance reached 1,500. The Van Nuys First Baptist Church, already huge, doubled in 10 years; as did the Dallas, Tex., First Baptist. Most of the 10 largest Sunday schools in America reached their great growth plateaus in the first 10 years of their history. Numerous small churches have doubled their attendance in three years and trebled it in five.

To isolate the factors which are responsible for great growth is difficult to do. However, here are some clues of differing value which may help to stimulate growth in your church.

1. The last vestige of *negative, impossibility thinking must be destroyed*. If not eradicated, it must at least be suppressed. An axiom worth memorizing is: *A church will grow to the degree that negative, impossibility thinking is replaced by radiant faith and creative optimism.*

Negative thinkers find ample reason to be convinced that church growth in their own church is not possible. What is worse is the amazing power of this negativism. It gallops like a prairie fire, sweeping away faith and optimism and leaving the scorched and blackened remains of a potential harvest in its wake.

It takes 10 positive believers to overcome the influence of one negative, impossibility thinker. Furthermore, the person who believes the church will not grow has nothing to do but sit with folded hands and wait for "nothing" to happen.

The optimistic believer in church growth has to couple faith with hope, love, and hard work. He has to persist and be willing to bear the weight of misjudgments when certain new ideas and new approaches do not result in visible growth patterns. When temporary failure withers the budding statistics, the impossibility people have many subtle ways of reminding the believers, "I told you so."

If the pastor happens to be convinced that substantial growth cannot be achieved, there is little the congregation can do to circumvent his unbelief. If, on the other hand, the pastor is a man of optimism and hard work and the congregation is made up of impossibility thinkers, then the pastor's first and foremost assignment is to *inspire faith where there is no faith.*

Faith is not born out of browbeating and berating from the pulpit the spiritually halt and maimed. As the Bible says, "The wrath of man worketh not the righteousness of God." Faith is not created by the preaching of ought's and should's. Faith is born of inspiration and example. One pastor alive with faith, hope, love, and hard work will, by the inspiration of his pulpit and his life, soon have around him a nucleus of optimistic church members whose faith has begun to be lifted. As believers grow themselves and see their church grow, their faith shines more brightly. It becomes increasingly harder for impossibility people to have a significant voice in the congregation. With a faith-inspiring pastor, the plague of disbelief dies quickly. However, both pastor and people may learn that doubt which has died has marvelous resurrection powers whenever the fear of failure begins to vibrate its hollow pipes.

The usual reasons given to support impossibility thinking are never new. People with mental blocks to faith are not inventive by nature. In an informal, nationwide poll of impossibility thinkers, it was found that the following reasons or excuses are most frequently offered by them as to why they think church growth cannot be achieved:

First is the excuse of a *bad location:* "There are too many Catholics, too many Jews, too many hippies." "The neighborhood is deteriorating." "The neighborhood is too sophisticated for our kind of church." "Downtown has had it." "The people we appeal to are too far away." "Everyone knows you can't build a growing church in this area." "If we were only on a main street!" "People cannot even come out around here after dark."

The second big excuse is an *inadequate building:* "The building is too small." "We don't have enough Sunday school rooms." "There is no place to park." "The hot weather is terrible and we don't have air conditioning." "The basement is poorly arranged." "The plans were outdated when the building was first put up." "The front steps are too high." "The lighting is poor." "We don't have pews."

If neither a bad location nor an inadequate building sounds convincing enough as a reason against growth, *lack of money* is almost always a clincher: "Our debt is too heavy." "The budgets are unfair for our size church." "The preacher gets paid too much." "We don't have any well-to-do people in our church." "All these new ideas cost money."

The final coup de grace intended to put to rest any urge to face the challenge of growth is an appeal to *the status quo:* "Why can't we leave things like they are?" "I believe in the old-fashioned way." "I haven't seen any of these ideas in the Bible." "All we need to do is pray and hold steady." "These new people won't understand how we do things." "The church is a place to worship, not a place to teach crafts and all these other things to children." "The best pastor we ever had here never did it this way."

2. The second factor in doubling church attendance is to *make every Sunday an event.* There should never be a ho-hum service or a Sunday that is just another day.

The first way to make Sunday an event is to give people the *red-carpet treatment.* Everyone who comes to your church is a wonderful person. He could have stayed home. No one made him come. Make him feel welcome. All growing, alive churches have happy bands of radiant Christian greeters at every entrance, and sometimes even in the parking lot.

One new man in town on a business trip told me he was greeted and his hand was shaken by nine different people between the front door of the church and his seat in the sanctuary. And he said there must have been 25 people who greeted him after the service.

Our church kept a red carpet which was rolled out on special days from the front door to the curb. Boy scouts opened car doors and ushered people onto the carpet of welcome. It is just the opposite of the experience a pastor and his wife had when they visited an Ohio church. They found the front door vacated and the foyer empty. After a moment a lady carrying a baby came through the swinging door from the sanctuary and looked at them in surprise: "Who are you," she asked, "strangers?" And she went on her way without another word or a gesture of welcome. Consider the importance of the people who put forth the effort to come to your church and then devise ways of welcome equal to your appreciation.

Series preaching both morning and night keeps continuity and adds another dimension of anticipation to the sermon and the service. Be sure, however, that the series will capture the imagination of the people. A dull, uninteresting series can hurt the level of expectation people have for a service. National headlines such as a moon walk, Middle East chain of events, elections, tragedies, and other captivating events can be used in sermon titles to help attract attention.

Special days call for special planning. For many years our church built the summer program around three focal Sundays, Memorial Day, Fourth of July, and Labor Day. At first the word to the people was, "Go ahead with your holiday plans, but for those who are going to be in town, we plan to make our services worth your while." After one summer, the best three attendances of the warm-weather season came on these holiday weekends. People learned to invite people, even from out of town, for these special Sundays. The days that could have demoralized attendance became days of highest morale.

The problem of long weekends is now compounded with the nine federal legal holidays. On the weekends of these special days, your church will either flourish or die, according to your attitude and preparation for them:

> New Year's Day
> Washington's Birthday—the third Monday in February
> Memorial Day—the last Monday in May
> Independence Day—July 4
> Labor Day—the first Monday in September
> Columbus Day—the second Monday in October
> Veterans' Day—the fourth Monday in October
> Thanksgiving—the fourth Thursday in November
> Christmas Day

Besides the federal holidays which must be redeemed by the growing church, there is a long list of other special observances proclaimed each year by the president. Since these proclamations result in public attention, the growing Sunday school or class may use them to advantage by finding ways to join this theme to the proclamation of the gospel. Included in these are the following:

> Senior Citizens Month—May
> Armed Forces Day—the third Saturday in May
> Law Day—May 1
> Mother's Day—the second Sunday in May
> Father's Day—the third Sunday in June
> Flag Day—June 14
> United Nations Day—October 24

Besides the national days which afford churches, and especially Sunday schools, a special theme, there are both local church, denominational, and Christian church year special days which, to an imaginative mind, suggest many ideas to help make such a Sunday an event. Among these are:

(1) Founders' Day: Use the date on the cornerstone for a special sermon and church observance.

(2) Pastor's Anniversary: Find an appropriate way to observe each anniversary of the pastor's first Sunday in the local pulpit.

(3) Any local community festivals with which the people identify

(4) School dates for "back to school," and graduation

(5) Family Altar Sunday, the first Sunday in January

(6) First Sunday in Lent

(7) Christian College Day, the last Sunday in April

(8) Baby Day, the first Sunday in May

(9) Mother's Day, the second Sunday in May

(10) Pentecost Sunday, the seventh Sunday after Easter

(11) Father's Day, the third Sunday of June

(12) Children's Day, the second Sunday in July

(13) Worldwide Communion Sunday, the first Sunday in October

(14) Laymen's Sunday, the second Sunday in October

(15) Reformation Sunday, the last Sunday in October

(16) Bible Sunday, the second Sunday in December

Finally, a list of special days would be incomplete without attention being given to eventful weekends, weeks, and months. Every church will make its own calendar, but here are some traditional times:

(1) Revivals

(2) Weekend events, such as "Three Great Days with the Bible"

(3) Youth Week

(4) Advent Season

(5) Holy Week

(6) Missionary Festival Convention

To review the above opportunities for special emphases, themes, preaching topics, advertising ideas, and church promotion might make it appear that every service is contrived. This is not true. For instance, all that needs to be done for Law Day is to ask an attorney in the congregation to pray the benediction. These special days and themes are to be the servant of the spiritual life of the church, not the masters of it.

The fourth way to help make every Sunday an event is the skillful use of special guests. A new voice adds variety, creates special interest, and often puts a new dimension into a day at church. The guests may be well-known or unknown. Here are four suggestions on how they may be used to enhance a Sunday in a local church:

(1) A guest teacher for a day in any adult class is usually a welcome change.

(2) An interview of a guest by the pastor in the night service keeps the time element in control and guides the topic of discussion.

(3) A one-minute report on some relevant matter or an alive testimony can help most services.

(4) A guest speaker, if he knows how to communicate, often makes an ordinary churchgoing experience a memorable event.

The fifth way to make every Sunday an event for families is to give special attention to children. Any church which demonstrates its love for children will be a growing church. Separate children's church services are good if the leadership is good. Scouts, cub scouts, choirs, singing groups, boys' and girls' clubs; ample, clean nurseries; and even children's bulletin boards are all ways to demonstrate love for children. Every child who participates enthusiastically in a church is like a magnet drawing in others.

The sixth and final suggestion toward making Sunday an event is the spiritual quality of all the services—Sunday school, morning worship, and night service. Music that inspires, preaching that helps people, special interest features, friendliness, and interest in children are basic factors. But above all, there must be a unique spirit of spiritual concern. Like the image of the iceberg, only a small amount of this spiritual concern is visible. Most of it is below the surface. But it must be there. Genuine love of people and concern for their problems as human beings spread among people like electricity. "People concern" may be mostly invisible but its reality is not denied. This concern is a chemistry of the soul that works irresistibly among people where it exists, spreading joy and drawing people to its source. Without it no Sunday will be an event.

3. There is a third factor necessary for doubling attendance in church. *The inexorable laws of Sunday school growth are not exclusive to Sunday school use, for they apply to all church events.* These laws have been articulated in many places, many times as follows:

a. A realistic attendance goal must be set. This may be based on the number of families now in the constituency of the church. It may include the number of people you honestly may expect to win in the next one, two, or three years. It may be based on a percentage increase over present attendance. It may be based on space available. It may be based on a survey of the community. Or it may be a goal handed down from some denominational body as your "fair share."

But one thing is crystal-clear and must be understood as an axiom: *No goal is meaningful until it is accepted and internalized by the people who are going to strive together to reach it.*

There are several characteristics of a goal which make it a tool for growth: (1) It must not be too easy or it will lose its challenge. (2) It must not be too high or it will bring discouragement. (3) It must be specific or it cannot be visualized. (4) A realistic time must be set for reaching this goal.

Some small churches can double their attendance in a few months or a year. A church of 50-100 might double in two years. Or a church of 100-200 might lay out a timetable and program to double in three years. The first year is the hardest. Once growth begins, continued growth comes more easily. And finally, (5) the goal must be broken down to enough small pieces to make every class and group a part of it.

b. An organizational pattern must be cut to care for the anticipated growth. Here is the axiom to memorize: *The size of the organizational pattern in a church will not insure growth but it will set a lid on how high regular attendance will go.*

Study the chart: "Organizational Patterns for Sunday School Growth." Read carefully the left-hand column, which indicates the number nearest to your attendance average for last year. Then read across the line to see if your organizational pattern is about the size indicated.

If you averaged 50 last year, you probably have the children and adults organized into two departments, one for children and one for youth and adults. And these people attend one of six classes.

If you want to double the size of your Sunday school of 50, take a look at the line which runs across the page from the 100 category in the left-hand column. To average 100, your school will need to be divided into four departments, one for preschool, one for children, one for youth, and one for adults. Then, instead of six classes you will have the pupils attending one of 12 classes.

To move from an average of 50 to an average of 100, the number of the departments must be doubled as well as the number of classes.

Because it is not practical to leap from an organizational pattern of 50 to 100 in one jump, it is better to first cut the

ORGANIZATIONAL PATTERNS FOR SUNDAY SCHOOL GROWTH

DEPARTMENTS

Attendance	Rooms	Department	Ages	Pupils	Classes
25	1	Children	(2-11)	10	2
		Youth	(12-17)	5	1
		Adult	(18 and up)	10	1
50	2	Children	(2-11)	19	4
		Youth	(12-17)	10	1
		Adult	(18 and up)	20	1
75	3	Preschool	(2-5)	12	3 groups
		Children	(6-11)	21	3
		Youth	(12-17)	13	1
		Adult	(18 and up)	29	2
100	4	Preschool	(2-5)	15	4 groups
		Children	(6-11)	28	4
		Youth	(12-17)	17	2
		Young People—Adult	(18 and up)	40	2
150	6	Nursery	(2-3)	9	2 groups
		Kindergarten	(4-5)	13	3 groups
		Primary	(6-8)	20	3
		Junior	(9-11)	23	3
		Youth	(12-17)	25	2
		Young People—Adult	(18 and up)	60	3
200	7	Nursery	(2-3)	12	3 groups
		Kindergarten	(4-5)	18	3 groups
		Primary	(6-8)	26	4
		Junior	(9-11)	30	4
		Junior High	(12-14)	18	2
		Senior High—Young People	(15-20)	26	2
		Young People—Adult	(21 and up)	70	3
300	9	Nursery I	(2)	9	2 groups
		Nursery II	(3)	9	2 groups
		Kinder-garten I	(4)	13	3 groups
		Kinder-garten II	(5)	14	3 groups
		Primary	(6-8)	39	5
		Junior	(9-11)	45	5
		Junior High	(12-14)	27	3
		Senior High—Young People	(15-20)	39	3
		Young People—Adult	(21 and up)	105	4
400	13	Nursery I	(2)	12	3 groups
		Nursery II	(3)	12	3 groups
		Kinder-garten I	(4)	18	3 groups
		Kinder-garten II	(5)	18	3 groups
		Primary I	(6)	17	3
		Primary II	(7-8)	35	5
		Junior I	(9)	25	3
		Junior II	(10-11)	35	4
		Junior High	(12-14)	36	3
		Senior High	(15-17)	32	3
		College-Career	(18-23)	40	3
		Young Adult	(24-40)	60	3
		Older Adult	(41 and up)	60	3
500 and over		Kindergarten through Junior will organize a department for each age or grade.			

organizational pattern for 75. For a 75 average, the number of departments is three and the number of classes is nine.

This same principle of workers involved in the organizational pattern applies to the Sunday church service attendance as well as to Sunday school. Billy Graham believes that the minimum attendance on a given night in one of his campaigns will be the total number of people in assigned jobs, multiplied by four. Below is an example:

2,500 in chorus choir
300 ushers
200 counselors
  50 miscellaneous personnel
3,050 people assigned jobs
× 4
12,200 total minimum attendance expected

If a church of 50 people has no choir and only a pianist, soloist, song leader, and two ushers part-time, besides the pastor, they are really doing exceedingly well to have 50 present.

What if that same church had a Sunday night choir of 16, an organist, pianist, and four full-time ushers, plus a children's group from a Sunday school class who put on a religious exercise of some kind? Even if the performance was not too good, the attendance would move upwards, naturally.

The number of persons in assigned jobs in the Sunday school of 50 is probably as follows:

1 superintendent
1 general secretary and treasurer
2 department supervisors
6 teachers
2 song leaders
12 total

If the 12 workers is multiplied by four, then the attendance is approximately 48. This formula will not always apply. (And there will be plenty of impossibility thinkers who will read this and proceed to show how it won't work in their church and Sunday school!) But, in general, the concept of growth by increasing the organizational pattern is right.

Another way of getting at the same concept is to take the number of Sunday school classes and multiply by 10. This does not work precisely, but the following table indicates there is a relationship between attendance and the number of classes.

Average attendance of 25 equals four classes.

Average attendance of 50 equals six classes.

Average attendance of 75 equals nine classes.

Average attendance of 100 equals 12 classes.

Average attendance of 150 equals 16 classes.

Average attendance of 200 equals 21 classes.

Average attendance of 300 equals 29 classes.

Average attendance of 400 equals 42 classes.

Do not be concerned if the formula or the arithmetic does not work out right. But memorize the axiom: *There is a direct ratio between the number of people involved in advance in specific participation and the total number of people present at any church event.*

c. The third inexorable law of church growth is more difficult to implement than either the first or second law: *Church growth is dependent on the square footage available for people use.*

A church with a sanctuary that seats only 50 people will have great difficulty trying to care for 150 persons. An attendance goal of 150 and an organizational pattern for 150 is useless unless the space can be provided.

SUNDAY SCHOOL SPACE REQUIREMENTS BY AGE				
Age-group	Sq. ft. per person	Maximum no. per room	Minimum sq. ft. or ft.	Maximum sq. ft. or ft.
Crib babies	25-35	12	200	420
One-year-olds	25-35	12	200	420
Two-year-olds	25-35	15	200	450
Three-year-olds	25-35	20	200	500
Kindergarten	25-30	25	300	600
Grades 1, 2, 3:				
Open room	20-30	25	300	500
Department assembly	8-10	40	200	400
Class	12-15	8	9 x 10	10 x 12
Grades 4, 5, 6:				
Department assembly	8-10	40	200	400
Class	9-10	10	9 x 10	10 x 12
Grades 7, 8, 9:				
Department	7-8	45		
Class	8-10	12	9 x 11	10 x 12
Grades 10, 11, 12:				
Department	7-8	45		
Class	8-10	15	10 x 12	12 x 13
Young People (Ages 18-23):				
Department	7-8	100		
Class	8-10	25	12 x 15	15 x 17
Adults:				
Department	7-8	100		
Class	8-10	25	12 x 15	15 x 17

A quick survey of the square footage chart indicates space requirements for doubling attendance. Follow these steps: (1) Determine the number of departments and classes needed to double the size of your Sunday school. (2) Compare this with available space in your present building.

Since almost all churches are short of space, here are a few suggestions for making the most of available space:

The easiest way for many churches to gain more space for children, and without cost, is to begin a Pastor's Bible Class in the sanctuary. Classrooms formerly occupied by adults may be taken over for children and teens while the pastor or some other qualified person teaches the adults. This space solution may be temporary and may raise other organizational problems, but it does open up additional room.

One of the most popular programs at the moment is multiple Sunday schools and services. This method of doubling space is excellent. It gives people an option on time for attending Sunday school and church. Twice as many people will have assigned jobs. It saves money on real estate, since the building gets double use. The problems in this approach are twofold: people who are conditioned to one Sunday school and morning service find it hard to re-program themselves; and second, there is no middle ground in moving to two sessions. You can't move into it gradually. All at once to get twice as many people to work is hard to do. But since there are no stages, this is the big hurdle to mount.

The only other option open to a crowded church is more space. Most of the time it means building. Sometimes the partitions can be rearranged within the building. In moving from 200 to 600 our church remodeled extensively twice without changing an outside wall. Other temporary alternatives include buying or renting adjoining houses or commercial buildings.

But, whatever the plan, the only way a church can be sure of being able to double its attendance is to be sure it has the necessary square footage for twice as many people as now attend.

Here is the axiom: *Although the total square footage in a church does not insure a full house, it sets the limit on how many people can be served.*

d. The next inexorable law of church growth is closely related to organizational pattern and square footage. *The people to fill the jobs on the expanded organizational pattern must be recruited and trained.*

If all the classes of a Sunday school were divided and

twice as many teachers of inferior quality were assigned to classes, the attendance graph would tumble while the level of friction among the people would increase. If the choir were doubled in size but with monotones, the results would be negative. If twice as many ushers were used, but all were untrained and did not possess a sense of the fitness of things, the result would be chaos.

There is nothing magic about growth by division. There can be death by division, too. Recruitment and training are twin essentials in expanded growth. What counts is to have more people recruited for training in their projected assignments. Choir members need to attend practice. Ushers need to be given an usher's manual and instructed. And Sunday school teachers need to be developed through an adult Christian education program which assures a level of ability in both attitude and knowledge.

e. The fifth *inexorable law of church growth has to do with visitation.* To make a visitation program effective, every church must find ways to handle the following five major problems:

(1) There is the *psychological* problem of accepting the visitation program on the same permanent basis as prayer meeting or any other spiritual function in the church.

(2) There is the *spiritual* problem of accepting witnessing as the New Testament norm for Christian service (Acts 1:8).

(3) There is the *organizational* problem of setting up a visitation system that makes sense to the people.

(4) There is the *mechanical* problem of assigning relevant calls and getting back pertinent calling reports.

(5) There is the problem of *motivating the people* to visit.

In this list of hazards which must be met in developing a useful program of visitation, technique and mechanics are of low priority while spiritual motivation is the highest.

One more thing needs clarification, and that is the purpose for visitation. A visitation program oriented to statistics for the purpose of formal or informal competition will not endure for very long. Congregations who visit to compete statistically with other congregations are trying to keep warm by a fire of motivation which gives off an uneven heat.

Visitation is the extended arm of the church in the community. Its purpose is to spread Christian sunshine and blessing into homes and hospital rooms. The purpose is ruined if people are nagged, criticized, or put on the spot about Sunday school and church attendance. The beginning of effective visitation is to be interested in people for their own sake, whether or not they come to church.

From a visit to the world's largest Sunday school, it was evident that operationally they did things like most other Sunday schools, but with much greater success. The tour guide explained the difference between this very large school (which was then in the summer slump with only 3,700 present) and most other Sunday schools. This formula for success can be written in three words on any 3 x 5 card. The first word is WORK. The second word is WORK! And the third word is WORK!!

With these people, work primarily meant visitation, which was done on a gargantuan scale. For churches that are being transformed from small to large, there is another three-word formula which also may be written on a 3 x 5 card. The first word is VISITATION. The second word is VISITATION. And the third word is VISITATION. Every pastor and superintendent might do well to roll up the windows of his car against the reactions of the curious and at least once each day raise his right hand over his head, clench his fist, and recite the magic formula: Visitation. Visitation! Visitation!! If the mental image of visitation could be implanted into the conscious and unconscious spiritual mind of every Sunday school administrator and teacher in the church, a spiritual revolution would begin!

THE FOUR
DIMENSIONS
OF EXCELLENCE

CHAPTER 10

Preaching to the Needs People Feel

Nothing can bring a Protestant church service to life and revive a dead church more quickly than good preaching. People go to hear preachers who have something to say that makes sense to them. Empty pews are soon filled when parishioners are convinced they can anticipate a good, helpful sermon week by week.

If all the laymen in all the static or dying churches could have one wish concerning their next pastor, it probably would be that he could preach. Bishop Kennedy said his most common request from church boards where a new appointment is imminent is, "Can't you send us a preacher? We have been without one for so long and surely we deserve one now."

The popular, column-writing psychologist, George W. Crane, said of pastors: "Many clergymen couldn't even rate a D in a high school public speaking class! You are an ally of Satan if you drive parishioners away from your church by your stodgy public speaking methods."

In spite of the need for good preaching there just aren't very many great preachers. History hasn't produced many Whitefields, Spurgeons, and G. Campbell Morgans. In one generation the churchgoers could count on one hand the preachers of the stature of Billy Graham, Norman Vincent Peale, and Peter Marshall. In any community there is only a small number of preachers who really communicate the gospel. But one thing is sure, their churches are growing.

Maybe this is the problem. Since a man realizes he cannot be eloquent even when he tries the hardest, then he simply quits trying. Since he cannot be a star in the constellation of preachers, he just fades into nothingness like a burned-out meteor. But in spite of all their failures at eloquence, many men go on trying and failing and feeling guilty.

One day I came to realize I couldn't be eloquent, and even more important, that I did not need to be. I stopped trying. But I didn't quit preaching. With a new enthusiasm I began working hard at developing my compassion and sensitivity to the needs of my people. With one or a small cluster of their needs in mind, I went with great concentration into the reservoir of God's Word to find what He had to say about them. Then, without notes and without any attempt to be scholarly, I talked directly to the people about their needs as they felt them and about what the Bible had to say concerning them.

This was a great turning point in my ministry, but a very difficult one. Old habits don't die easily. Trained in a tradition that placed great priority on doctrine, I found myself using the pulpit to prove my doctrinal soundness by answering questions no one was asking. My so-called Bible sermons grew out of the pages of commentaries instead of the needs of the people. With only two years of doubtful Greek in college, I tried to show fine discriminations of interpretation by reference to the Greek, of which I knew precious little.

Then there came the academic stage. Following a Ph.D.

program, I began to throw academic goofy dust into the air on Sunday mornings while the congregation stagnated. I quoted the authorities with authority. But, as might be expected, there was a loss of authority in the message.

There have been three great epoch-making events in my ministry. The first was my call to preach, which still is fresh and never has wavered. The second was the day I died out to people and position, the day I literally was cut free to do a job in the name of Christ. I actually loved the church and its leaders more when I was liberated from an inordinate concern for its hierarchy. I actually loved all the people in my congregation more—even those in the pastor's "loyal opposition"—when I was saved forever from a bondage to their opinions. And the third great event in my ministry was the day I started preaching sermons to *help* people, not *impress* them. Since I had started preaching concepts instead of words, my notes were no longer needed. I found that the most helpful sermons were preached from my heart to theirs about a subject or a problem both of us knew firsthand. I tried to show God's solution.

I still wrote out my sermons in longhand, but they were much simpler. Gone were the impressive quotes and the abortive attempts at tossing out stardust. As much as possible, I memorized the scripture passage. I began the sermon with several anecdotal attempts to identify the problem in human experience. Then came the text or longer passage of scripture in as accurate and modern application as possible. Then followed the body of the sermon, which was a series of related ideas which flowed naturally from one to another. Invariably the conclusion was a challenge to do something about it.

This is my way of preaching. It is not necessarily the best, but it fits me. Not all should try to emulate it. But there are some helpful suggestions that can make any good pastor-preacher a better one. An itinerant preacher has got to be a specialist in speaking. But a pastor-preacher has to wear well. He has the advantage of continuity. He can be loved, not just admired. Through service in critical times of human experience he can build bonds to the people of the congregation which are cemented with moments of deep emotion that enhance every sermon thereafter in the minds and hearts of those whom his hands and his heart have served.

1. Since the pastor-preacher is going to be in the same pulpit next week, he does not have to push people toward a given response this very moment. He need not be argumentative or overpowering in his approach. He can omit heavyhanded pressure. His sermon is just a verbal expression of his continuing love and concern for the people.

2. The pastor-preacher can speak loudest through his own character and ideals. The most persuasive speakers are those who represent in their own persons both what the people in their congregation *are* and what they would *like to become*. They do not need to master a set of speaking techniques as much as they need to master themselves. The good preacher must first be a good human being.

3. The pastor-preacher speaks best when he identifies most fully with the feelings of his own flock. The deep strength of Abraham Lincoln's power over his own and successive generations lay in the fact that he was a man of the people. The pastor-preacher both exemplifies and transcends the people he serves.

4. The truly persuasive pastor-preacher is one who is honestly and deeply attached to the underlying ideals of the ordinary people in his church. He values them so deeply and understands them so truly that they come alive in his mind and feelings, and there grow and develop. This becomes "the heart" from which he speaks.

5. The persuasive pastor-preacher speaks with authority from all the power and optimism the Bible affords for

human needs. He is not a biblicist. He does not treat the Bible like a book of magic. He does not try to use theological clichés to answer the great human issues. He allows the Bible to be its own Authority to human need.

6. The pastor-preacher does not pressure people, because he knows human nature will not change until it is ready to change. People will not even hear or listen until they are ready. They will see what they wish to see and hear what they wish to hear. Pressure only builds defenses. The pastor-preacher understands all about the foolishness of preaching. He depends on the Holy Spirit, who has His own way and sense of timing.

CHAPTER 11

The Place of Music
in the Church

Church and music are inseparably bound together! This has been true from the beginning of the Old Testament. After Moses and his company came through the Red Sea on dry land, they paused for the first thanksgiving service on record. And the main feature of that service was an original song written for the occasion by Moses' sister, Miriam. When King David led the people in a great worship service, there were (according to the Bible record) more than 4,000 singers and musicians in the choir and orchestra. The Book of Psalms, which is one of the most beloved books in the Bible, is actually a hymnbook.

The New Testament continues to underscore the place of music in religion. Over Bethlehem the angels sang for the birth of Jesus. In Jerusalem, Jesus concluded the Last Supper by the singing of a hymn. In Philippi, Paul and Silas sang in their own private service while they sat secured in the stocks of the local Roman prison.

Paul not only sang himself; he admonished others to do so. To the Colossians he wrote, "Let the word of Christ dwell in you richly in all wisdom; teaching and admonishing one another in psalms and hymns and spiritual songs, singing with grace in your hearts to the Lord." To the Ephesians he wrote, "Be not drunk with wine wherein is excess; but be filled with the Spirit . . . making melody in your heart." And to the Corinthians he said by way of personal testimony, "I will sing with the spirit, and I will sing with the understanding also."

Not only is music at the heart of the scriptural record of worship, but music has been a major factor in every great revival movement. Congregational singing was important to the Protestant Reformation. As Luther gave the Bible to the people in the language of their day, he also gave them the gospel through hymns which they could sing both in church and at home. Some Catholics who feared Luther most cried that "his songs have damned more souls than all his books and speeches." Luther undertook the composition of the German song, "that the Word of God might be preserved among them if by nothing else, by singing."

Singing was also vital to the Wesleyan Revival in Britain and America. Charles Wesley has given us the gospel in the singing page. John not only wrote songs himself but edited all that were published by Charles and himself. These singing preachers not only taught their people what to sing but also wrote out detailed instructions on how to sing in church. They sold their songbooks at prices the common people could afford. The songs and their use in congregational singing gave the revival a thrust it could not otherwise have had.

In more modern times, music and evangelism still go hand in hand. Great evangelists like Billy Sunday and Billy Graham are joined with equally great musicians like Homer Rodeheaver, Cliff Barrows, and George Beverly Shea. Gypsy Smith said, "I have never seen a crowd get blessed of the

Lord until first they cut loose and sing in the freedom of the Lord." Haldor Lillenas said, "The song service is not merely an introductory prelude to the . . . service; it is indeed a part of it." It has been affirmed that "after the Bible . . . nothing is more important to the people than its hymnology. If one is forced to choose between the privilege of preaching what the people are to believe or teaching them the songs they will sing, he might do wisely to choose the latter."

Music has ever been at the heart of evangelism. There is not a growing church anywhere that is not known as a singing church in its community.

What direction should we go in our church music? Some would have us "lift the level of our people" by making the Sunday service an experience in music appreciation. Others would set the gospel to toe-tapping music which mimics the rhythm of the world if not its spirit. There are times when our appreciation of fine church music needs to be lifted, and there are times when rhythmic gospel tunes are appropriate. But somewhere between these two opposites will be found the true fulfillment of the purposes of church music. Here are five suggestions:

1. Music in the church is at its best when emphasizing the basic doctrines. The Catholics of Rome were shocked by the doctrine of Martin Luther, but they were absolutely terrified by the power of his music.

2. Our music is at its best when it helps to create a spiritual atmosphere in the service. We believe there is an atmosphere in evangelistic churches which is unique. That atmosphere doesn't just happen; it is created. Although many things make their contribution to this spirit, a major factor is music. The grace of knowing what to do next in revival music is a rare gift. The capacity to sense the mood of the congregation, to invest a situation with the right kind of songs and choruses, even to know when to stop, is an art which needs cultivating.

3. The music of the church should help people to get in touch with God. Worship and evangelism are not opposites. They are one and the same thing. Music which helps the saint to see through the windows of heaven will help the sinner to be convicted. The Holy Spirit, who brings blessings to one person, brings deep conviction to another—and perhaps through the same song. The Christian life is in harmony with God and spontaneously bursts forth into singing. Not all of the redeemed are singers, but all of the redeemed have a song. There is wide variety in music expression and appreciation. It is better to allow for a wide variety in our revival music. The logic of Gypsy Smith makes sense at this point: "Please, let me have the hymn that says something to my poor heart."

4. Music is at its best in a revival atmosphere. Some churches may excel in the presentation of cantatas, anthems, and oratorios, but evangelistic churches come into their own in gospel music.

5. Effective music in evangelism combines musicianship with a personal testimony—singing and playing the testimony of a gospel song backed by the power of the Holy Spirit. The influence of music over the hearts and wills of human souls is beyond question. That is why sacred music has always had a prominent part in evangelism. Its purpose had been to augment the preaching of the Word and move the hearts of men. It is also a means for drawing people under the sound of the gospel. People are attracted as much by happy, unrestrained enthusiasm in music as by anything else. But music in evangelism is of little value apart from the spirit of those who participate. The only music which moves the hearts of men and women is music by musicians inspired by the Holy Spirit.

But all the responsibility for good gospel music in the church does not lie with the musicians. Too many pastors and evangelists seem detached, or disinterested, or bored with the so-called preliminary part of the service, while they wait for the two important parts of the service, the offering and the sermon. Perhaps it is fitting to conclude with the five rules John Wesley gave to his preachers concerning congregational singing:

1. "Sing all. See that you join with the congregation as frequently as you can. Let not a slight degree of weakness or weariness hinder you. If it is a cross to you, take it up, and you will find it a blessing."

2. "Sing lustily and with good courage. Beware of singing as if you were half dead or half asleep; but lift your voice with strength. Be no more afraid of your voice now, nor more ashamed of its being heard than when you sang the songs of Satan."

3. "Sing modestly. Do not bawl, so as to be heard above, or distinct from, the rest of the congregation, that you may not destroy the harmony; but strive to unite your voices together, so as to make one clear melodious sound."

4. "Sing in tune. Whatever tune is sung, be sure to keep with it. Do not run before, nor stay behind it, but attend closely to the leading voices, and move therewith as exactly as you can; and take care that you sing not too slow. This drawling way naturally steals on all who are lazy, and it is high time to drive it out from among us and sing all our tunes just as quick as we did at first."

5. "Above all, sing spiritually. Have an eye to God in every word you sing, aim at pleasing Him more than yourself, or any other creature. In order to do this, attend strictly to the sense of what you are singing; and see that your heart is not carried away with the sound, but offered to God continually; so shall your singing be such as the Lord will approve of here and reward when He cometh in the clouds of heaven."

What can be done to continue and increase the degree of excellence in music in a given local church?

1. Let the people be themselves. Forcing a different kind of music on people against their will or tradition confuses and irritates them.

2. Be slow in reducing the standard of church music to the idiom of the day. Wesley and Luther wrote songs plain people could enjoy. But the text of those songs was full of sound doctrine. And the melodic line was strong enough to endure until the present day. If the only difference between the music in church and on the stage is the words, then the rhythm and shallow musical sentiment of the world have invaded the sanctuary, youth choirs perhaps excepted.

3. Guide all soloists and groups to sing and play as well as they are able. Sloppy preparation, omission of practice time, and last-minute choices of songs tend to encourage people to testify before the song is performed as an initiative move to detract attention from the lack of excellence.

4. Most small churches would do well to build their entire music ministry around the hymnal. It is economical since "special" books are expensive. The quality of the music in both text and melody is guaranteed. There is great variety for all kinds of solos, duets, mixed quartets, and choirs for almost any occasion. The best way to improve the quality of music in small churches who cannot afford large music budgets is to stick to the hymnal and put their money in a good grand piano.

CHAPTER 12

The Miracle and Power
of the Printed Page

Except for the Holy Spirit, the greatest possession of the Church has been the miracle and power of the written Word.

It has been said that when religion went west across the Allegheny Mountains, through the hinterland of the middle prairies, and finally along the Santa Fe and Oregon trails to the west coast, it was the Baptists who went first. They accompanied the trappers and fur traders, and many times were the trappers and fur traders themselves. The Methodists went west when the trails were established for their horses, and their circuit riders became legendary. The Presbyterians went west when the roads would accommodate the wagons which contained their libraries. And the Episcopalians went west when the Pullman was added to the railroad. However true to the facts this might be, it is at least certain that from the schoolhouse revival in Appalachia to the cathedral on Nob Hill in San Francisco, the basic tools of the Church have been and are the Bible and the hymnbook.

From the beginning, the Church has invested the Word with more than ordinary meaning. John, who addressed his Gospel to the Greek philosophers as well as to the Hebrew theologians, used the idea of the Logos to explain who Christ is. He opened the fourth Gospel with the strong affirmation: "In the beginning was the Word, and the Word was with God, and the Word was God" (John 1:1). He then added: "And the Word was made flesh, and dwelt among us" (John 1:14a).

The Apostle Paul used the miracle and power of the written Word to further explain the meaning of the Word that became flesh. His 12 letters and one note (Philemon) were copied and circulated among the churches with more than ordinary efficacy. When the Spirit appeared to John on the isle of Patmos, the command from God was plain: "What thou seest, write in a book, and send it unto the seven churches" (Rev. 1:11).

But the written word in the Early Church was more than prose; it also included poetry set to music. From what Paul had to say about music, it is evident he had confidence in its power as an expression of the gospel. He saw music as the alternative to evil when he wrote to the Ephesians: "And be not drunk with wine, wherein is excess; but be filled with the Spirit; speaking to yourselves in psalms and hymns and spiritual songs, singing and making melody in your heart to the Lord" (Eph. 5:18-19). To the Colossians he wrote: "Let the word of Christ dwell in you richly in all wisdom; teaching and admonishing one another in psalms and hymns and spiritual songs, singing with grace in your hearts to the Lord" (Col. 3:16). And to the Corinthian church, set down in the center of the Las Vegas of its day, Paul wrote: "I will sing with the spirit, and I will sing with the understanding also" (I Cor. 14:15b).

In the light of this emphasis on the word, it is no exaggeration to say the greatest mechanical invention of all time, for the furtherance of the gospel and the church, is the printing press. When a little known monk, who was short of stature and generally mild and academic of manner, nailed a list of 95 discussion questions on the door of the Castle Church in Wittenberg, he set in motion the currents of the great Reformation movement which not even the monolithic power of the papacy could stop. Historians who have analyzed the factors which made this worldwide religious movement possible have called attention to the Renaissance, to the rising tide of nationalism—not unlike the tides of nationalism in the world today—and the discredited leadership of the papacy. But they all agree that the greatest single tool in the Protestant Reformation was Gutenberg's printing press. Luther's voice could be stopped, but his books and his Bibles could not. Finally on an April evening in 1521, three years and six months after posting his first questions, Luther stood before the emperor of the Holy Roman Empire, not to be charged with the heresy of preaching, but to be faced with a stack of his books. The miracle and power of the printed page had stirred the hearts of the common people and had stopped Rome dead in her tracks.

Luther, like Paul, knew the two-sided power of the written word, both in prose and in poetry set to music. He wrote the marching songs of the Church and filled them with his theology.

> *A mighty Fortress is our God,*
> *A Bulwark never failing.*

Not only did Luther write 36 hymns himself, but before he died, 60 separate editions of hymnbooks were published under his direction. It is no wonder that his enemies said, "His songs have damned more souls than all his books and speeches."

The miracle and power of the printed page were recognized by John and Charles Wesley. A book, William Law's *A Serious Call to a Devout and Holy Life*, was a factor in the conversion of John Wesley. And the evening John dropped in at the prayer meeting on Aldersgate Street his heart was strangely warmed, not by the preaching of a sermon, but by the reading of a book. Wesley had just come from a service in St. Paul's Cathedral, where the impact of choir, organ, preaching, and Christopher Wren's architecture are traditionally massive. But his heart was not warmed in a unique way until in the prayer meeting someone read from a book —from the preface of Luther's commentary on Paul's letter to the Romans.

Wesley was an omnivorous reader and he became a voluminous writer. He is often quoted as saying, "Let me be a man of one book." But to one of his preachers who boasted that he never read any book but the Bible, Wesley said, "If a man read only his Bible, he would soon cease to read that." John and Charles wrote, edited, or otherwise were creatively involved in 453 separate publications which ranged all the way from a four-page tract to a multi-volume commentary.

On the day after his conversion, Charles Wesley wrote his first gospel song, "Where Shall My Wondering Soul Begin?" On the first anniversary of his conversion he wrote "Oh for a Thousand Tongues to Sing." And for the rest of their lives, John and Charles collaborated on song sheets, and hymnbooks, publishing and republishing them right down to the end. Of these early Methodists it has been said, "Though preachers have sometimes gone a little astray, the hymns have brought the people back."

Dr. P. F. Bresee said a minister should do three things: He should have a good library, should memorize the books of Isaiah, John, and Hebrews, and then should soak himself in the old hymns of the Church. He admonished ministers to preach out of minds that were full and hearts that were aflame.

The mind of man is a marvelous computer. If man were to build a computer to do everything the mind can do, it would take a building at least as large as the Empire State Building to house it and at least half of all the power from Niagara Falls to run it. Even then, says one scientist, it is doubtful if man's computer could do all the things that can be done in the compact, little package man carries with him everywhere he goes. The mind can recall things that happened five, 10, 25, or 50 years ago, if one has lived that long. It can recall in black and white, or in color. And if the experience was particularly enjoyed, the mind has the capacity of an artist to embellish it and make it more enjoyable on the replay than it was live. The mind can gather data, sort, assimilate, synthesize, identify trends, and extrapolate just as the computer can.

But beyond this, the mind can do more than the computer. The mind can gain insight and understanding. The mind can be moved upon by faith (see William James, *The Will to Believe*), and the mind can be cleansed and filled with the power of the Spirit. There may be, as Paul put it, "the mind of Christ" in you. Jesus told His disciples that "the Comforter, which is the Holy Ghost, whom the Father will send in my name, he shall teach you all things, and bring all things to your remembrance." It is very comforting to know that the Holy Spirit will enlighten one's mind and activate one's memory.

Another factor in understanding the soul is human emotion. The emotions of man are that part of the immortal soul which has feelings. Certainly animals have the emotions of anger and fear, and in some instances can develop an amazing sense of loyalty to one person. But only man has the capacity of empathy. Only man can structure, and feel, and see, and even experience something from another person's point of view. Man often understands with his emotions even when his mind cannot grasp the reason why.

Then, too, the soul of man involves the will. The will of man is perceived as the seat of transgression: "Sin is willful transgression of a known law." Sinful acts are executed by the will, but it is the mind and the emotions which motivate the will to act sinfully. In the new birth, sins of the will are forgiven; but in the experience of entire sanctification the mind, the emotions, and the will are cleansed.

Now the miracle of music and prose is its appeal to the inner self of man: his mind, emotions, and will. Bread and butter will feed this organism, and the fleshly passions will satisfy its basic drives. But man cannot live by bread alone, and the level of life's expectation is not met with sex, alcohol, and money. God has made us for himself, and we never can be satisfied until the needs of the soul have been met.

Certainly the publishing business is not the only agency dedicated to meeting the needs of the souls of men. But it is a fact that no mechanical invention has equaled the miracle and power of the printing press. Our choirs practice, our congregations sing, our preachers study, our laymen learn, our children memorize, our minds are enlightened, our emotions are moved, and our wills are activated through the materials that are turned out by the printing press.

This is where one more dimension of excellence enters the local church. The aggressive church encourages its people to buy and read good periodicals and good books.

The pastor's bookshelf or the book table in the foyer of the church can be a great supplement to the pulpit in the sanctuary and the podium in the classroom. Good as the spoken word may be, the written word is better, because it can be studied.

Dr. Elton Trueblood says, "The presence or absence of a book table is coming to be something of a revelation of the quality of concern in a local Christian fellowship." There are still many who have not caught the idea, but most effective congregations now keep their book tables going every week. The result is marvelous, for laymen are now discussing books and ideas which used to be the property of the clergy only.

Church libraries are good if properly located and supervised. But the actual sale of good books to learning Christians is better. An owner prizes a book more because of his investment in it. And congregations whose members are building up personal libraries are usually building up in other ways.

A false, idolatrous attitude toward the sacredness of brick and mortar has kept some churches from this excellent ministry. Every church must solve this problem in its own way. Some people feel that buying a book to read a message is little different from putting money into a collection plate to hear one. The major point is to find a way, whatever it may be, to distribute good books and periodicals among the congregation. It adds a dimension of excellence to the total ministry of the local church.

CHAPTER 13

The Ministry of Ushering

Any act of Christian service which helps direct men into fellowship with Jesus Christ is a ministry. The most prominent ministry in the Church is *preaching*. Although the Apostle Paul referred to it as "the foolishness of preaching," he also wrote to the Romans, "How shall they believe in him of whom they have not heard? And how shall they hear without a preacher?" (Rom. 10:14) Even in churches which have set the pulpit to one side and have made the altar the center of worship, preaching still is the most prominent part of the service.

The second prominent ministry in the Church is *teaching*. Next to the preaching of the gospel, Martin Luther believed teaching was the highest calling of mankind. Teaching is mentioned many times in the New Testament and included among the spiritual gifts. The pastor who preaches without teaching, or the church which evangelizes without instructing, is not only obscuring the cross of Christ but failing to provide the Holy Spirit with opportunity for one of His most important functions: "He shall teach you all things, and bring all things to your remembrance, whatsoever I have said unto you" (John 14:26). "He will guide you into all truth" (John 16:13). In one of his letters to Timothy, Paul said, "The servant of the Lord must . . . be gentle unto all men, apt to teach, patient; in meekness instructing those that oppose themselves" (II Tim. 2:24-25).

The third great ministry in the Church is *music*. According to Paul, music is at least on an equal plane with teaching as a ministry in the Church: "Let the word of Christ dwell in you richly . . . teaching and admonishing one another in psalms and hymns and spiritual songs" (Col. 3:16). The importance of the Holy Spirit in the ministry of music was further emphasized in his correspondence with the Corinthians: "I will sing with the spirit, and I will sing with the understanding also."

The fourth great ministry of the Church is *ushering*. Paul, who believed in the power of preaching, the importance of teaching, and the ministry of music, also wrote, "Let all things be done decently and in order" (I Cor. 14:40). The importance of the usher's ministry caused one pastor to say, "If I had to choose between losing the ushers or the choir, I would rather lose the choir." This probably was an exaggeration used to emphasize the importance of the ministry of ushering in his church, but it is a fact that it will take music from a very extraordinary choir to overcome the poor work of inefficient ushers. In fact, it probably is true that all four of these ministries interact on a fairly equal basis in any given local church. Though of unequal importance, preaching, teaching, singing, and ushering are all so closely related to each other that one does not tend to rise above the other. The preachers, teachers, musicians, and ushers all need each other!

In the Old Testament Tabernacle, and later in the Temple, ushers were called doorkeepers. The Psalmist, who wrote to the chief musician in the Temple, understood the importance of ushers when he said, "How amiable are thy tabernacles, O Lord of hosts! . . . Blessed are they that dwell in thy house: they will be still praising thee. . . . I had rather be a doorkeeper in the house of my God, than to dwell in the tents of wickedness" (Ps. 84:1-10). One of the functions of doorkeepers in the Old Testament was to receive the collections from the people: "Go up to Hilkiah the high priest, that he may sum the silver which is brought into the house of the Lord, which the keepers of the door have gathered of the people" (II Kings 22:4). The Old Testament Chronicler wrote to Shallum and his brethren who "were over the work of the service, keepers of the gates of the tabernacle . . . keepers of the entry" (I Chron. 9:19). And in Ezekiel's vision of a future temple, he saw space reserved for the priests, the musicians, and two sets of ushers: "the keepers of the charge of the house," and "the keepers of the charge of the altar" (Ezek. 40:45-46).

In the New Testament, the Temple ushers were given unusual authority, evidently as uniformed guards. In the Acts of the Apostles, "the captain of the temple" and "the officers" are referred to several times in connection with arrests and general handling of the crowds. It was these doorkeepers, or ushers, who carried out the orders of the high priests in the persecutions in the Temple against the apostles immediately following Pentecost, and 30 years later in the arrests and maltreatment of the Apostle Paul.

Jesus used His disciples for the functions of ushers on many occasions. They prepared the way for His coming; they introduced people to Him, and in general directed the people who had come to hear Him speak or to be touched by His healing hands. On one occasion, Jesus gave a sharp warning to the disciples, who as ushers had endeavored to keep children away from the Master. On still another occasion, Jesus directed the disciples in organizing a congregation of 5,000 men plus women and children, to be seated in groups of 50. Then, with Christ supplying the unending loaves and fishes, the disciples served the hungry multitude.

It was among the functions of the first church board to serve as ushers: "Then the twelve called the multitude of the disciples unto them, and said, It is not reason that we should leave the word of God, and serve tables. Wherefore, brethren, look ye out among you seven men . . . whom we may appoint over this business. But we will give ourselves continually to prayer, and to the ministry of the word. And the saying pleased the whole multitude" (Acts 6:2-5). The character of these first deacons is spelled out clearly. They were (a) men of honest report, (b) men full of the Holy Ghost, (c) men full of wisdom, and (d) men full of faith. This means, then, that Stephen, the first Christian martyr on record, was both a member of the church board and served tables daily as an usher or deacon.

The three qualities of good men explained by Jesus in the Sermon on the Mount could not be more applicable than they are to the ministry of church ushers. First, the ministry of ushering is like salt, which makes everything more palatable and which serves as a general preservative against deterioration. Jesus did not say, "Ye ought to be the salt of the earth," but He said, "Ye are" (Matt. 5:13). Ushers enjoy the ministry of a constructive influence. Paul said, "Let your speech be alway with grace, seasoned with salt" (Col. 4:6). A good usher adds a tang of joy to a churchgoer's Sunday morning experience instead of a tinge of drabness. Also, the ministry of an usher is like salt because salt can never do its work until it is brought into close contact with the substance on which it is to exert its influence. The church ushers, pastors, musicians, or teachers come into direct contact on an individual basis with more people in a given service than anyone else who ministers to them. The ministry of salt is silent, inconspicuous, and sometimes completely unnoticed. But it is there—in a powerful and useful way.

Also, a good usher is like "a city . . . set on an hill" (Matt. 5:14). While ushers are like inconspicuous salt, they also may become like a city on a hill. They become landmarks to churchgoers who learn to depend upon them. Stability helps overcome many other weaknesses in the priority of qualifications among ushers. The first glimpse of an usher on whom a churchgoer has come to depend brings an internal sense of welcome repose: Someone is on hand who is interested in me! It is not uncommon for an usher to become an adviser, a source of information, counselor, or better yet, an intermediary between the needs of a specific person and the resources available through the pastor, musicians, and teachers of the church.

Third, a good usher is like a lamp on a stand, not put "under a bushel, but on a candlestick; and it giveth light unto all that are in the house" (Matt. 5:15). A lamp brings warmth and welcome to all who are in the room. One flickering candle can brighten the conversation in a room and bring an inner feeling of warmth and joy. As a lamp dispels the darkness and brings emotional warmth to a room, so the ministry of an usher can make a similar intangible contribution to all who experience the inner light of pleasure in people which he allows to shine through himself.

Jesus concluded this discussion on the character of a good usher by saying, "Let your light so shine before men, that they may see your good works, and glorify your Father which is in heaven" (Matt. 5:16). It is the nature of Christian character to radiate; it cannot help but shine. But the radiance of this glory is not for "self" but for the kingdom of God. The ministry of an usher is not intended to bring glory to himself but to God. Just as a pastor preaches in the Spirit, and the musician sings in the Spirit, the usher must do his work in the power of the Holy Spirit—bringing glory to God in the Lord's house on the Lord's day.

One day in Chicago, Mr. Wrigley looked mournfully down upon the streams of customers who stood before the ticket boxes at Wrigley Field to get refunds for the baseball seats which they had bought but could not locate. While Mr. Wrigley groaned inwardly about the loss of his customers, Andy Frain, a young man in his early twenties, approached the financial wizard and begged for the job of head usher at the great baseball stadium. Destitute for a solution to his problems, Wrigley hired him.

In only a few days Andy Frain completely revolutionized ushering at Wrigley Field and made himself "King of Ushers." Even more important, he made ushering a respectable new vocation. Mr. Frain organized a school for his men whom he had handpicked from many applicants. He gave them blackboard drills and showed them training films. At the completion of his training, each recruit had to pass a test and serve as an intern for two weeks of fieldwork. Only then did he recieve a diploma and the resplendent blue uniform with brass buttons and gold stripes.

In a few years Andy Frain had expanded his ushering to include many of the great auditoriums and arenas in the United States. In a single year, his ushers handled crowds equal to the entire population of the United States. Through his branch offices in every major American city, Mr. Frain supervised every large gathering in the nation. Even the Democrats and Republicans agreed on one thing: Andy Frain's ushers would handle the crowds at both national conventions.

While the need for good ushers has been recognized and met in the large secular auditoriums, the need for good ushers is being recognized more and more by the leading clergymen. Even two generations ago, Dwight L. Moody was particular about his ushers and personally hired the 500 men who were to seat the crowds for the revival meeting he held in New York City. In current city-wide revivals no little attention is given to the need for efficient ushering. Large crews of volunteer men are recruited and trained in advance both to care for the seating of the people and to assure the smooth operation of the invitation. In churches, small and large, clergymen more and more are relying upon efficient ushers for smoothness in meeting the individual problems which relate to the handling of the congregation. There are four reasons for the importance of ushering:

1. To begin with, *the usher is often the first official representative of Jesus Christ seen by people entering God's house.* Teachers meet the people in the religious education classroom. Pastors face the people from behind a protecting pulpit after everyone is in his place. Choir members sing with their eyes fastened on the director, not the people. But before members of the congregation ever see the pastor, the musicians, or even the teachers, they come face-to-face with a church usher. The attitude which the usher communicates to church members and friends helps set the tone for everything else which is to happen. As an official representative of the church and of Jesus Christ, the usher has an enormous obligation in helping lead people into readiness for learning, worshiping, and evangelism.

2. *The church usher may be the only individual contact the church makes directly with persons during their attendance in a service.* Preachers, teachers, and musicians minister to people in groups, while ushers minister to people only as individuals. A Spirit-directed word of encouragement, reassurance, or kindness may be the most significant ministry some people receive in their entire church attendance experience. Only a few can linger to meet the pastor, to ask questions of the teachers, and to talk with the musi-

cians, but everyone may have a firsthand encounter with the usher.

3. *The usher is the only person whose functions cannot be replaced or omitted.* Preaching in a given service has been omitted. There have been services without choirs, and on occasion classes have been dismissed. But there is no substitute for the work of ushers in any church service, regardless of its character. In weddings, funerals, Communion services, evangelistic campaigns, patriotic rallies, cantatas, Christmas plays, films, and any other kind of church meeting, ushers are important.

4. *An usher is a forerunner.* As John the Baptist was a forerunner for the ministry of Jesus Christ, the church usher is a forerunner for all the other ministries in the congregation. The attitude the usher demonstrates in the foyer of the church is a forerunner of the ministry to be experienced in the sanctuary. An usher in the vestibule can enhance or detract from the ministry in the chancel by the way he administers his own duties.

An Usher's Prayer

"May I, dear Lord, in church today, fulfill my assignment in a Christlike way. Make me efficient in what I do, effective in what I say, understanding in the way I feel about people, and helpful in the attitudes I have toward them. Make me a co-worker with the pastor, the church musicians, the teachers, and most of all, Lord, with Thee. Save me from hurtful words and harmful deeds. Make people glad they came to our church today because the Holy Spirit ministered to their needs through the sermons and prayers of the pastor, through the music of the organist and singers, through the explanations of understanding teachers, and through the ministry of ushers like me. In Christ's name. Amen."

An Usher's Commission

"At the beginning of another year the church gives you

this fresh commission, new and yet old. Allow the hospitality of this church to become incarnate in you. Wrap every word and clothe every action in the spirit of human kindness. May your kind of Christianity help people to let down their guards, open their hearts, and relax their minds for the worship of God and the direction of His Holy Spirit. Be understanding with the difficult person. Exercise compassion with all kinds of people. Learn to be efficient, but not at the expense of kindness. And accept from the pastor and congregation this assignment which ranks in importance with the other major ministries of this church. May your highest good be the kindness of human understanding, your greatest virtue the stability of a man in Christ, and your most effective tool the indwelling presence of the Holy Spirit."

FINANCING
THE LOCAL
CHURCH

CHAPTER 14

✓ Managing the Church Finances

_____

There are four great priorities in the pastor's assignment: *First,* he is to proclaim the gospel of Jesus Christ through *(a)* preaching, *(b)* teaching, and *(c)* man-to-man conversations. *Second,* the pastor is to organize the people for growth. This includes *(a)* personal spiritual growth, *(b)* growth in the strength of the internal structure of the church, and *(c)* growth in the size of the church. *Third,* the pastor makes plans for Sunday in church to be the biggest event of the week for the entire family. *And fourth,* the pastor is to finance the entire church program adequately.

In a local church these four priorities are interlocking. They all depend on each other. In the specialized ministry of an evangelist, missionary, or Christian college teacher these four factors are not so prominent. But in the year-after-year work of the local pastor his effectiveness will rise or fall on the level of his ability to preach, organize, promote, and manage the finance. No local church program will survive long that is not adequately financed.

The long-term effectiveness of the pastor's financing of the local church depends on two factors: (1) his ability to inspire the people to give, and (2) his management and control of the funds to be expended.

The first characteristic of a pastor who successfully finances the local church is his proven ability to manage his own financial affairs. The church who wants a pastor who is capable of financial leadership may learn quickly about a prospective pastor's ability to do that job in the church by checking his personal financial record. Does he have a tendency to overspend? Are his bill-paying habits orderly? Does he always have his hand out for a free ride, or at least a discount? Does he whine and complain over money matters?

If a man lives within his income and saves enough to make some small investment in his own old-age security, he will likely lead the church into an orderly financial program.

Probably the best single index of a man's financial ability is the way he takes care of some kind of minor investment. A penny saved is not necessarily a penny earned, but a penny invested is, if the investment is wise.

The pastor who lives in a state of financial crisis needs professional help as much as a person with disturbed emotions. Pastors' salaries are low! Let's accept that as fact! But this is no excuse to be slovenly and uncaring in personal finances. Irresponsibility is unforgivable in a pastor's personal bank account. He is not expected to have lots of money, ever. But he is expected to be a good steward of the money he does have.

There are many useful ideas on responsible personal financial policies, but here are a few selected thoughts that have helped our family:

1. An old preacher told Mrs. Parrott and me in our first year in the pastorate, "If you buy all the things you think you need, you will never have any money." Impulse buying is the bane of the financially undisciplined.

2. The only way to tithe is to take it right off the top, first, before any other disposition is made of the weekly income. And the only way to save money is to save systematically and invest it somewhere beyond the temptation to spend it. My father taught me early that it would always take all my salary to live on, regardless of increases. As salary increases, more demands are made on the pastor. Therefore, any savings would have to be taken out systematically, just like tithing.

3. The only way to keep your self-respect and hold your head high is to pay your own way your fair share of the time. The graciousness of generous members and friends is to be deeply appreciated, but the pastor who presumes on their goodnesses is eroding his own spiritual leadership.

4. Debt within limits for long-term investment can be healthy hedging against inflation and old age. But debt for current family operating expenses is disastrous. Maybe one contract at a time on an appliance or car can be handled within the family budget without strain. But because of low salaries, the pastor's family who has several time-payment commitments at once is probably building for a crisis when some unexpected expense shows up without warning.

5. Financial pressures on the pastor's family follow a life cycle. *First* is the fairly light financial period before the

first baby is born. The salary may be low but so are the expenses. And it may be the minister's wife will be working while school bills are being paid off and furniture bought. During the *second* period, which covers the raising of children, the financial burdens increase gradually to a great crescendo during the years children are in college. Then, during the *third* period, the load lightens with children grown, and for many pastors the best income years are at hand. Personal finance is no easy matter during any of these stages. But money matters can be managed in such a way that the pastor's family will be kept out of a continual money crisis.

After learning to manage his own affairs, the pastor's next concern is management of church finances. *And management of church finances begins with a good budget tool.* The church that spends what comes in without a budget to cover all needs is like the irresponsible person who spends his entire paycheck on the weekend without thought of the following five days.

The first items to be considered in the budget are the pastor's salary and the budgets for missions, Christian education, and the district. Write these in first. When church boards have resisted this approach, they need to be reminded that little sympathy can be generated for them if the pastor's salary and the budgets are behind. When these are not paid on time, the tendency of the people is to complain that the salary is too high and the benevolent budget unfair. But if the money runs out before the mortgage and the light bill are paid, the pastor has considerable leverage for raising the funds. Have the board put a motion in the minutes that the pastor's salary and the budgets for missions, Christian education, and district interests be declared Class A items and paid first, with all other bills and obligations declared Class B items.

There are several kinds of church budgets. Some are

unified, including all monies of all departments and auxiliaries. Others are all-inclusive, covering the total expenditures of the church but none of the auxiliaries such as Sunday
school. There is considerable argument, however, for a
minimum operation budget. Such a budget includes *all
the expenditures to which the local church is obligated.*
There are several special characteristics of this kind of
budget.

1. It includes only what has to be paid to meet current
obligations. It does not include the Sunday school and world
missions. These two needs are financed separately because
they have special motivational capacities.

2. It does not include special projects such as revivals
and building projects, which should be self-supporting.
These are in-and-out items and are reported separate from
the current operations budget.

3. One advantage of this kind of budget is simplicity
of explanation. Every Sunday the Counting and Banking
Committee gives the pastor two primary figures: *(a)* income
on the current operations budget, and *(b)* all other project
income, itemized.

4. When the entire amount of the minimum current
operations budget is projected for the year, it is divided
into 52 equal amounts. Then this amount is multiplied by
four or five, according to the number of Sundays in the
month. These amounts should be raised each and every
month of the year. The church thus has 12 minor crises instead of one big one at the end of the year. If on the last
Sunday night of the month there is still a shortage, the need
is presented to the congregation. No hands are raised, no
pledges taken. Everyone is asked to pray and give as God
directs.

5. With the minimum budget met each month, the

extra money which comes in above the budget is banked against the day of special need.

Here are the steps in building a budget:

Step one: *List the categories of church expense.* These may vary from one church to another. Add to or take from the following suggested list of minimum expenses:

1. Salaries
2. Benevolent budgets, exclusive of world missions
3. Taxes
4. Mortgage payments
5. Insurance
6. Youth activities
7. Cleaning supplies
8. Building maintenance
9. Utilities
10. Flowers
11. Conventions
12. Bonuses and gifts
13. Office equipment and maintenance
14. Postage
15. Office supplies
16. Printing and advertising
17. Tithe envelopes
18. Music
19. Contingencies

Step two: *Determine the costs on all expenditures in these categories for last year.* A few phone calls and a little legwork will soon produce these figures from the suppliers. This information must be accurate.

Step three: *Project the increases or decreases for expenditures in all of the categories of the budget for the year at hand.* In preparing the budget for the board and the congregation, it is good to identify three figures as follows:

Categories of Expense	Expenditures Last Year	Projected Increase (Decrease)	Proposed New Budget
Salaries			
Benevolent budgets			
Taxes			
Mortgage payments			
Insurance			
Youth activities			
Cleaning supplies			
Building maintenance			
Utilities			
Flowers			
Conventions			
Bonuses and gifts			
Office equipment & maintenance			
Postage			
Office supplies			
Printing and advertising			
Tithe envelopes			
Music			
Contingencies			

Step four: *Divide the total budget figure by the number of Sundays in the year* and multiply by four or five according to the number of Sundays in each month. Three important figures will become very familiar: (1) amount needed per Sunday, (2) amount needed in a four-Sunday month, and (3) the amount needed in a five-Sunday month.

Step five: *Present the budget to the church board for approval before presenting it to the church.* Ordinarily, the budget is put together by a budget committee appointed by the pastor. It may or may not be useful to ask the congregation to vote on accepting the budget.

Step six: *Go out on a limb of faith and declare that no month shall close without meeting the total budget.* There have been times when the budget was met in stride with considerable excess. And there have been other times when the church board has been called for special prayer on the last

Sunday afternoon of the month. Once the momentum is gained, the people will find great joy in seeing that this monthly need is met.

The size of the church and the economic circumstances are not important. The ingredients of success are a clear-cut goal and spiritual motivation to meet it. People are not motivated to give by pressure and shame, but by inspiration and blessing.

Besides mastering his own personal finances and developing a good budgetary tool, the pastor has other financial concerns. *He needs to work with the church board in developing a list of projects to adopt if and when additional money comes in above the minimum budget.* These might include:

1. New sound system
2. Prayer chapel
3. Storage cabinet
4. Additional rest room
5. Audiovisual screen
6. Chapel carpet
7. New church sign
8. Additional property

Another responsibility of the pastor is to develop good accounting procedures. It is best to have the counting and banking of the money handled separately from the treasurer, whose responsibilities are to keep the books and write checks. Your local banker will be glad to give you free professional guidance in setting up these procedures so a good audit may be made annually. For the protection of everyone involved, an audit is a must each fiscal year.

And finally, the pastor can lead the church board in developing controls on spending. The best procedure is to appoint someone as purchasing agent with authority derived from the board to sign vouchers and issue purchase order numbers. Almost any business organization will help you set up a system of controls. But whatever the system, there must be one. Otherwise the spending will tend to get out of control and the budget becomes a useless piece of paper.

In summary, the financial needs of the local church can be met with spiritual joy and can be seen as a means to expanding the kingdom of God, if the following factors are operating:

1. The pastor must put his own financial house in order.
2. The minimum amount of money needed for financing the church must be determined.
3. The money must be raised each month to meet the budget.
4. All items not in the budget must generate enough motivation among the people to pay their own way.
5. Good accounting procedures and spending controls must be developed and put to use.
6. Money must always be looked upon as a means to an end and not as an end in itself.

CHAPTER 15

How Tithing
Is Misunderstood

Tithing is one of the most misunderstood words in the English language. Most people have missed what tithing is all about. It has been thought to be an unfair, worrisome, burdensome scheme thought up by some pious Old Testament Jews and latched on to by modern-day pastors as a way to get the bills of the church paid. Maybe this overstates the fact, but even so, some fundamental misunderstandings about tithing do exist.

First of all, *the very origin of tithing is misunderstood.* Abraham and his nephew Lot were rich ranchers. Their cattle and sheep ranged for many miles in all directions from their homeplace at Hebron. Contention arose over grazing land. The sheepherders and cowpunchers who worked for Lot became very nasty in their dealings with the herdsmen and cowboys who worked for Abraham. So the two men agreed on a division of the land which gave the well-watered plains of Jordan to the young man, Lot.

However, soon after he moved into his new prosperity, a band of five cattle rustlers who lived beyond Damascus saw an opportunity to steal from Lot. In the fracas which resulted, they not only took the sheep and cattle of Lot but kidnapped him also.

Abraham organized a posse of 318 men, who, under heavy arms, chased the marauders to the Euphrates River beyond Damascus. They rescued Lot and retrieved all the plunder. Coming back into their home territory, Abraham, Lot, and all the riders were met by the priest Melchizedek, who provided them with the substances for a service of thanksgiving. And as recognition of God's blessing upon him, "Abraham gave tithes of all." Although giving in recognition of God's blessing is recorded in the experience of Cain and Abel, almost at the beginning of written history, this reference in the fourteenth chapter of Genesis is *the first specific mention of tithing in the Bible*.

This idea of tithing was passed on from generation to generation. After Jacob, who was Abraham's grandson, received the paternal blessing of his father, Isaac, he left home to seek a wife and to make his fortune in Mesopotamia. On his first night out, he camped along the trail. While looking at the stars, the question came to him, Will the God of my grandfather, Abraham, and of my father, Isaac, be with me also? Jacob fell asleep with this question on his mind.

As he slept, Jacob slid into a deep dream in which he saw a ladder from earth to heaven with angels ascending and descending. While he looked, God appeared at the top of the ladder giving him the promise of His presence. He said, "Behold, I am with thee, and will keep thee in all places whither thou goest, and will bring thee again into this land; for I will not leave thee, until I have done that which I have spoken to thee of" (Gen. 28:15).

At the end of his dream Jacob awoke and said, "Surely the Lord is in this place; and I knew it not." He went back to sleep again; but when he got up the next morning, Jacob took the stones he had used as a pillow and made an altar to God. He changed the name of the place from Luz to Bethel. And then he made a vow about tithing: "And this stone, which I have set for a pillar, shall be God's house: and of all that thou shalt give me *I will surely give the tenth unto thee*" (Gen. 28:22).

Tithing continued to be a concern of the early patriarchs until the time of the Exodus. Then Moses on Mount Sinai got a message from God, loud and clear. The tithe was no longer to be merely a voluntary act, but a part of the principles of godly living. Here is a record of the commandment God gave to Moses: "*And all the tithe of the land . . . is the Lord's:* it is holy unto the Lord. And if a man will at all redeem ought of his tithes, he shall add thereto the fifth part thereof. And concerning *the tithe of the herd, or of the flock,* even of whatsoever passeth under the rod, *the tenth shall be holy unto the Lord. . . .* These are the commandments, which the Lord commanded Moses for the children of Israel in Mount Sinai" (Lev. 27:30-34, emphasis mine).

Throughout their history as a chosen nation under God, *the children of Israel were tithing people.* As they accepted the lordship of Jehovah, they expressed gratitude in the systematic payment of their tithes. The writer of the Proverbs caught this when he said, "Honour the Lord with thy substance, and with the firstfruits of all thine increase: so shall thy barn be filled with plenty, and thy presses shall burst out with new wine" (Prov. 3:9-10).

By the time the system of worship had been established following the experience of the children of Israel at Mount Sinai, tithing was a central principle of religious living. *Tithing was not so much a matter of commandment as it was of blessing.* Listen to the words of Azariah, the chief priest, who said this about tithing: "Since the people began to bring the offerings into the house of the Lord, we have had enough to eat, and have left plenty: for the Lord hath blessed his people; and that which is left is this great store" (II Chron. 31:10).

Even the same prophets who strode through the length and breadth of Palestine calling the people to repentance also called them to pay their tithes. Malachi was one of those men who called things like he saw them. The prophets never were known for hedging on an issue. Malachi just accused a man who did not pay his tithe of stealing from God: "Will a man rob God? Yet ye have robbed me. But ye say, Wherein have we robbed thee? In tithes and offerings. Ye are cursed with a curse: for ye have robbed me, even this whole nation" (Mal. 3:8-9).

But Malachi does not close with a negative accusation about the delinquent tithers. He closes the Old Testament with one of the most triumphant, blessed promises in the Book. Every tither loves this promise and has proved it in his own life: "Bring ye all the tithes into the storehouse, that there may be meat in mine house, and prove me now herewith, saith the Lord of hosts, if I will not open you the windows of heaven, and pour you out a blessing, that there shall not be room enough to receive it" (Mal. 3:10).

From this quick examination of tithing in the Old Testament several things should be clear to us. *First,* what a man gave to God in recognition of His blessing was a significant matter. *Second,* Abraham, Jacob, and others in the Old Testament opened up a new era of religious living when they adopted tithing as a way of life. *Third,* tithing was not only a clear-cut commandment given by God to Moses on Mount Sinai, but it was the royal road to blessing and productivity in both church and family finance.

Tithing has also been misunderstood in relation to the teachings of Jesus. Some have found un unstable comfort in the fact that Jesus did not make any outright commands concerning tithing. This is true; He did not. However, He did more than just restate the commandments of the Old Testament in cold, objective language. He fused the brittle, unbending commandments of the Old Testament with the new motivation of New Testament love.

Look at the Sermon on the Mount (Matthew 5). Jesus did not begin His declaration on the meaning of His kingdom by restating the Ten Commandments. He opened with seven principles for happy living. (Actually, "blessed" in the original language means *happy*.) The Ten Commandments were written in negative language. Jesus gave the Beatitudes in a positive, optimistic tone. He told His followers seven ways they could be happy. None of these directives from Jesus were negative. These were ways to cope with life without losing one's optimism.

In the second paragraph of His sermon, Jesus said that Christians are "the salt of the earth." They are not the scum, but the salt, which gives tang and flavor. He continued by saying they are "a city set on an hill" and "the light of the world." And He added that this light is not to be hid under a bushel but to be put on a candlestick to bring a glow to all who are in the room (Matt. 5:13-16).

Then in the third paragraph of this great sermon, Jesus deals once and for all with the matter of the commandments. It seems like He could see His followers getting anxious and uneasy when the basis of religious living was shifted from negative keeping of rules to the positive fulfillment of them through the principles of joy and love.

Jesus said, "Think not that I am come to destroy the law, or the prophets: I am not come to destroy, but to fulfil. For verily I say unto you, Till heaven and earth pass, one jot or one tittle shall in no wise pass from the law, till all be fulfilled. Whosoever therefore shall break one of these least commandments, and shall teach men so, he shall be called the least in the kingdom of heaven: but whosoever shall do and teach them, the same shall be called great in the kingdom of heaven. For I say unto you, That except your righteousness shall exceed the righteousness of the scribes and Pharisees, ye shall in no case enter into the kingdom of heaven" (Matt. 5:17-20).

Jesus then lifted out four illustrations from the Old Testament to show what He meant by the fulfilling of the law. The first was the commandment against murder. He said, "Ye have heard that it was said by them of old time, Thou shalt not kill; and whosoever shall kill shall be in danger of the judgment."

Then He went beyond that law when He said, "But I say unto you, That whosoever is angry with his brother without a cause shall be in danger of the judgment."

His second illustration was on adultery. He said, "Ye have heard that it was said by them of old time, That thou shalt not commit adultery."

But He fulfilled that law by saying, "But I say unto you, That whosoever looketh on a woman to lust after her hath committed adultery with her already in his heart."

The commandments are not true because they are in the Bible, but rather they are in the Bible because they are true. God did not reach out arbitrarily to pick up certain laws and make these His commandments. But, rather, He put into the code of Moses those laws that are basic to human nature. Long before the laws of Moses were ever written on Sinai, Cain was accused by his own built-in prosecutor and tried to rationalize his brother's murder. And long before the Levitical law on worship was ever put down on parchment, including the law concerning tithing, Abraham, Jacob, and others were tithing because it was the right thing to do in honoring God's blessing in their lives.

Now I wish Jesus might have chosen tithing for one of those illustrations on the fulfillment of the law. If He had, I wonder what He might have said. Without being presumptuous or irreverent, it might have gone something like this:

"Pay ye your tithes in the beginning. And then give generously of your offerings, that ye may prove to your Father in heaven that money does not dominate you for selfish reasons. Give the Heavenly Father the opportunity to bless you because you give your tithes and offerings out of love, systematically, in the church where you attend."

Third, tithing is misunderstood for what it does in the church and in the family. People who travel the wheat country of Kansas, Nebraska, the Dakotas, and the Canadian prairies are often struck with the stark outline of a little country church against the sky. A man in one of these little country churches was asked to serve as treasurer for the new year. His church had been unpainted and weather-beaten for years. At certain times during the storms the roof leaked. The congregation had only a part-time pastor, who also served three other congregations. The people in general were discouraged and nothing was happening.

This man, who operated the local granary, finally agreed to be treasurer of the church for the new year if the congregation would promise not to call for any accounting of the funds until the entire year was finished. Since they were a small church and knew each other well, everyone agreed to this proposition.

Only a few months after the new church year had begun, the treasurer began to make suggestions to the board on improvements which could be done on their church with the surplus in the treasury. Shocked that there should be money available, they finally took his word for it that the balance was indeed in the bank. That year they painted the church, and put on a new roof. They put more gravel on the parking lot and built a nice, white fence around the entire compound. They brought in a full-time pastor. And when the report was given at the end of the year, they learned that the church had been generous in its contributions to missions.

Amazed that their church could achieve so much financially in a single year, they pressed this marvelous new treasurer to learn the secret. They were all aghast when he told them that his secret was plain and easy. He said, "All of you bring your grain at harvesttime into my granary. When I figured up how much I owed each one of you, I just deducted 10 percent for the church and gave you the balance without ever saying anything about the deduction. You lived happily and got along well on the nine-tenths, and God's work in our community has prospered more this year than ever before since we have lived here."

It is a fact that when the church is a tithing church unusual things begin to happen. We believe in a praying church, a spiritual church, a calling church, and a loyal church, but the most sure way to transform a church and the people in it is for every wage earner in the congregation to become a tither.

That is why the Apostle Paul wrote to the church in Corinth about systematic giving. He said, "Now concerning the collection . . . Upon the first day of the week let every one of you lay by him in store, as God hath prospered him, that there be no gatherings when I come" (I Cor. 16:1-2).

Not only are the needs of the church cared for when we tithe, but the financial needs of the families who tithe are also met. No study has ever been made which would compare the standards of living in a congregation between those who tithe and those who do not. But it is a fact that no tither would feel that he could live better if he did not give so much to God. Instead, he has long since learned that the fulfillment of the law in tithing comes when giving is done systematically, generously, and from a heart of love to God.

THE PASTOR
AND HIS
PEOPLE AS
COUNSELORS

CHAPTER 16

✓ Who Makes a Good Counselor?

Whether we like it or not, every pastor and pastor's wife is a counselor. And whether they want to be or not, every youth worker and most Sunday school teachers are counselors, even perhaps against their wishes. Among those professionally trained for counseling or the "amateurs," who makes the best counselor? The writer of Proverbs said, "Counsel . . . is like deep water; but a man of understanding will draw it out." Christian counselors who possess the capacity to draw out the best in people are priceless tools of God. If many people suffer from the lack of Christian counselors, perhaps an equal number suffer from the hands of so-called Christian counselors who do not understand people or the counseling process.

A researcher named Fiedler found that "even laymen can describe the ideal therapeutic relationship in terms which correlate highly with those of the experts." In other words, he found that the layman who has never been exposed to the long training of the professional counselor still has a very good idea of the kind of person the counselor should be if he is going to be of help to the people who visit him. He further found that the best qualities in a good counselor were those qualities which made him an acceptable human being in general.

Here are some characteristics of the Christian who makes a good person to visit when in need:

1. He has an underlying regard for the inherent dignity and worth of every human being.

2. He helps make people feel wanted and needed.

3. He treats everyone fairly.

4. He genuinely likes people and accepts them as they are.

5. He has deep and enlightened personal convictions, but does not pretend to know more than he does.

6. He encourages individuals to work through their own problems and to arrive at their own decisions.

7. He is sensitive to the needs of young people and respects their confidence.

8. He is stable and mature.

The characteristics of a good counselor are illustrated in the relationship of Jesus to His disciples. Jesus did a superb job of counseling the Twelve, because He gave them a sense of security, He manifested a strong confidence in their abilities, and was patient with their faults and failures. He loved them without condescension, which made it possible for Him to rebuke them. He did not overlook social and economic problems, but He worked most to give an inner transformation that would give them freedom in a hostile world. He was patient, even to the point of kindness, toward one whom He knew was a betrayer. In Him the Christian counselor finds his highest Ideal.

The prime characteristic of a good Christian counselor is a confident personal faith. This assumes a satisfactory experience of forgiveness and cleansing. It also assumes a day-to-day devotional relationship with God. Further, the Christian counselor must be in harmony with the spirit of the people and the theology of the church where he works. No Christian counselor is ready to involve himself in the lives of people unless his own faith is secure.

Above all, a Christian counselor is a wholesome human being. In describing the person who helps them, people are likely to mention such human qualities as, "He is considerate and thoughtful," or, "He is a real person." They are also likely to say, "He's a regular guy," "He is so easy to talk to," or, "He listens to me, all the way through."

Gilbert Wrenn from the University of Minnesota suggests that the nature of the counselor himself is a more important factor in counseling than any of the procedures he uses. "The personality and reputation of the counselor," he says, "may be more important in determining counseling outcomes than the procedures he uses. The procedures merely sharpen and make more effective the kind of person he is."

In the Christian counseling situation this simply means that people will not seek help from Christians in whom they do not have confidence as human beings. As in the case of Deborah in the Old Testament, the Christian counselor will be sought out only if respected as a person. If in the opinion of people the Christian counselor has been a competent, thoughtful, and sensitive leader, one who has shared deeply and richly in life, he will have overcome one of the biggest hurdles in counseling.

According to Dr. Erickson, former dean of the College of

Education at Michigan State University, the most important characteristic of a good counselor is to be "an active, interested listener." These two adjectives, active and interested, in one sense, seem contradictory. But persons have presented problems to a counselor who, though he was outwardly listening, was inwardly disinterested. He was actively thinking of something unrelated to the person and his problem. But to be an active, interested listener means one who is concentrating with mind, eyes, and even emotions on the person and the problem at hand.

Listening, then, is an indispensable asset for the person who is a counselor. A listener shows more interest in others than in himself. The good listener asks few questions; he speaks only to maintain the flow of conversation. A skillful listener seldom makes comments, gives little advice, and above all does not talk about his own experiences and beliefs. This requires patience and practice. The tendency of most Christians trying to help people in a one-to-one situation is to talk too much. Almost all Christians want to preach. Unless disciplined to listen, they will deluge the person and bury the problem in an avalanche of verbiage.

Hamrin, an authority on counselor training, writes of a young man who claimed to be a good listener. With permission, Dr. Hamrin recorded one of the young counselor's interviews. When the interview was analyzed, it was found that the young man talked 92 percent of the time, listening to the other person only 8 percent of the time. Most people, including Christian counselors, are unconscious of the extent to which they tend to dominate a conversation.

Good listening during a counseling session serves several purposes. One function is *catharsis*—the release of pent-up feelings in the individual. The person who expresses his feelings of anger or guilt to an understanding listener is more likely to be emotionally healthy than those who do not. Bottled-up emotion is the pressure tank which eventually explodes in havoc. One of the functions of a counselor is to help a person express his negative emotions without hurting himself or someone else.

A second reason for listening is *to better understand the other person.* Unless the counselor learns to read feelings, he can never understand the problem as the other person sees it. The importance of this listening process is emphasized in a book for professional counselors called *Listening with the Third Ear.* Theodore Riek sees the process of listening behind the spoken word as an indispensable tool in counseling effectiveness.

Further, having a willing listener seems to work counseling wonders for people. Many people have experienced times when it seemed that their own thinking was fuzzy until they began to tell their problems to some understanding person and suddenly the picture became clearer. Most Christian counselors who have learned to listen and ask a few questions have often been rewarded by hearing a person say, "Now I think I understand something I didn't see before." Actually, the counselor has done nothing more than provide himself as a sounding board for the expression of the thoughts and feelings of a troubled human being.

Emotional maturity does not mean that the Christian counselor is not to have feelings of his own, or is to suppress his feelings. It means that *he should recognize and control his feelings.* Nor does emotional maturity mean that the Christian counselor is not to display emotion in dealing with people. Emotional dullness is a counseling liability, because few people are attracted to a colorless counselor. Enthusiasm and aliveness are as much assets in counseling as in teaching or preaching. Dynamic personalities attract people, both young and old. Being alive unto God and alive to people go together like electric wires and light bulbs.

It is too much to expect the counselor to be free from personal ideas and prejudices. But the counselor must at least be able to direct the expression of his feelings. His prejudices should not affect his attitudes toward the other person he is trying to help, regardless of his problems or appearance.

The helpful counselor shows respect by listening attentively and indicating that he understands. But he never expresses shock or surprise. If the teen-ager, red-faced and angry, says, "I hate my parents," the wise counselor will say, "Tell me about it." If the counselor shows shock by saying, "Oh, my, that's terrible!" the teen-ager will either withdraw and tell no more or enter into a performance planned to *really* shock the counselor. By controlling his own emotions, the counselor helps the other person to express his. By not censuring and by not moralizing, the counselor helps the person to feel that he is accepted even if his behavior is not.

The Christian counselor must be consistent in all areas of his life—in the home, on the street, in the classroom, in the pulpit, in the parking lot, as well as in the counseling session. A pioneer who once lived along the Oregon Trail wished to have fine neighbors around him. He set out to choose people whom he thought he would like to have settle nearby.

On the trail near his home the pioneer posted a sign which read: "Strangers, stop awhile and refresh yourself."

Many weary people, westward bound, stopped in response to this invitation and then were engaged in conversation by the old pioneer. He would ask them where they were from, and next how they liked it back there. If their answer was negative and they affirmed that they were glad to leave the place where the neighbors had been mean, selfish, and hard to live with, the old pioneer shook his head and said, "Well, that is just the way they are around here too."

But if their response indicated that the neighbors had

been fine, gracious, and courteous, and that the travelers left reluctantly and only because of the possibility of greater opportunity in the West, the pioneer would nod his head and say, "Well, that is just the way the people are around here too." Then he would proceed to help that individual and his family to find a place nearby, for he wanted such as his neighbors. He realized that one's attitude and skills in dealing with friends are transported from one environment to the next. The counselor cannot be one person in dealing with people who come for help and another in the other areas of his life. Emotional maturity or immaturity affects all of his life.

According to the psychologist George Lawton, the well-adjusted counselor is one who:

1. Is willing and able to assume the responsibility appropriate to each age or period of life as he reaches it.

2. Participates with pleasure in the experiences that belong to each successive age level, neither anticipating those of a later period nor holding on to those of an earlier age.

3. Accepts willingly the responsibilities and experiences that pertain to his role or position in life, even though he may object to his role.

4. Attacks problems that require solution instead of finding means to evade them.

5. Enjoys attacking and destroying obstacles to his development and happiness once he has decided that they are real and not imaginary obstacles.

6. Makes important decisions with a minimum of worry, conflict, advice-seeking, and other types of running-away behavior.

7. Abides by his choice until new factors of crucial importance enter the picture.

8. Accepts the authority of reality; that is, he finds the major satisfactions of life in accomplishments and experi-

ences that take place in the real world and not in the realm of daydreams and make-believe.

9. Draws lessons from his defects instead of finding excuses for them.

10. Does not magnify his successes or extend their application from the field in which they originally occurred.

11. Knows how to work when working and play while playing.

12. Is able to say, "No," to situations which provide temporary satisfaction but which, over a long period, run counter to his best interest.

13. Is able to say, "Yes," to situations that are momentarily unpleasant but ultimately will aid him.

14. Is able to show his affection directly and to give evidence of it in acts that are fitting in amount and kind to its extent.

15. Is able to endure pain, especially emotional pain or frustration, whenever it is not in his power to alter the cause.

16. Has his habits and mental attitudes so well organized that he can quickly make the essential compromise called for by the difficulties he meets.

17. Is able to bring his energies together and concentrate them effectively on a single goal, once he is determined to achieve it.

18. Realizes that life is an endless struggle in which human purposes are hurled against external resisting forces and realizes that, in this struggle, the person who fights himself least will have the most strength and the best judgment.

The ideal Christian counselor who measures up fully to all these ideals probably does not exist. However, the effective counselor will have a degree of the emotional and spiritual maturity which the above ideals indicate; at least they will be his goal.

The Apostle Paul said, "I will sing with the spirit, and I will sing with the understanding also." *An understanding spirit, desirable in everyone, is absolutely necessary for the Christian counselor.* People seek money, fame, and position in their efforts to make themselves attractive to others, when they could realize their goal more quickly by developing an understanding spirit.

To understand the other person, it is necessary for the counselor to put himself in the other person's place, to try to feel as he does, to see things as he sees them. Understanding does not mean sympathy, which is a poor substitute for seeing things from another's point of view. Sympathy may only encourage self-pity, the most ruinous of all sentiments. But every human being has a deep need to be understood.

Suppose Mary comes to the counselor all upset because her mother and father would not allow her to stay out on dates with a visiting sailor until 2 a.m. The counselor might inwardly label her parents as old fogies. But that would not be understanding Mary. On the other hand, the counselor might agree with the judgment of Mary's parents. Would that help to understand her? No. The main point in understanding Mary is to attempt to see the problem through her eyes, exactly as she sees it, with the same emotions and limitations of judgment. This is a difficult technique, but it can be learned.

Seeing through the eyes of the other person means that the counselor must concentrate on accepting the other person as he is. In current writings on counseling, less stress is being put on specific techniques and more on the counselor's attitude. Dr. Bordin says, "More and more stress is placed upon 'understand' which means getting inside the client's frame of reference, seeing his phenomenal world as he sees and experiences it."[1]

To assume the other person's point of view demands courtesy and respect. It requires the conversation to be at the level of the counselee's emotional and intellectual development. The counselor should not expect the teen-ager, for instance, to display mature restraint and understanding beyond his years and experience. Upset people tend to regress in their emotional competence.

Luke said of the prodigal son, "He came to himself." The prodigal's capacity to "come to himself" is God-given. The battle many counselors have is in their own faith in the other person's capacity to see things himself and make responsible decisions. The counselor must decide, Do I have enough faith in this person to believe he has the capacity for self-direction or do I basically believe that his life would be best guided by me? The counselor must concentrate on one purpose only: that of providing deep understanding and acceptance of the attitudes manifested by the other person at the moment. At the same time he must have faith that God will help him "come to himself," if he is given time to talk out his problem sufficiently with a person who does not criticize him but tries to see the problem just as he does.

Jesus was once presented with a woman taken in adultery. After dispersing the crowd with a well-timed rebuke, He turned to her and said, "Neither do I condemn thee: go, and sin no more." The pastor in the pulpit may strike out against evil in every form, but in the counseling situation there is no faster way to cut off the flow of conversation than for him to express an attitude of condemnation.

The counselor may despise sin but he must love the sinner. Dr. Erich Fromm says that the final test of love is whether the counselor can love the "stranger in his gates." He defines the stranger as a person who holds a different set of behavior standards from the counselor's. This acceptance of the person does not mean that the counselor must set aside his own values and adopt those of the "stranger." People in general tend to appreciate others who have the same likes and dislikes as themselves, and tend to reject persons whose opinions conflict with their own. This kind of love may endure on Main Street or in the Congress, but it fails miserably in the counseling room.

Jesus asked, "If ye love them which love you, what reward have ye?" In the counseling situation, none! Love that sinner; don't try to be his judge. This is true regardless of how he behaves, or what he confesses, or what beliefs he holds. Leave the judging to God. Let your role be that of the helping hand.

Another characteristic of a good counselor is his *courage to be honest with himself and others concerning the strengths and limits of his abilities.* He is not driven by a need to pretend or to be arrogant in showing how much he knows and how right he is. The good counselor has humility, but it is humility rooted in strength, not in weakness. Humility is not a way of deploring one's own lacks, but a way of recognizing realistically how much one can do and cannot do.

A wise counselor recognizes that some people have problems too deep and complex for him to attempt to help solve. Such cases he refers to a qualified specialist trained to handle particularly difficult situations. It is generally best for the lay counselor in the local church to refer people first to the pastor, who may then make the formal referral to a community agency or trusted professional.

The counselor in the local church ordinarily confines his work to people who are able to continue their daily routines, who do not manifest symptoms of mental illness, and who are already making a reasonably good adjustment to life. He is limited in time, experiences, training, and understanding and should recognize his limitations.

Here is a list of some of the symptoms which indicate the kinds of problems which Christian lay counselors may detect in people who need professional help:

1. A person needs special attention who reports sensations of tingling or numbness in various parts of the body. The numbness may often be in an arm, a leg, or the side of the face.

2. A chronic refusal to eat and a continued complaint against most or all food.

3. Twitches of the facial muscles, tremors, or muscular spasms.

4. A person who seems to have no sense of right or wrong.

5. Severe speech disorder or muscular disturbances, convulsions, epilepsy, and even momentary periods of losing consciousness.

6. Migraine headaches.

7. The person who suffers from either of two extremes: delusions of grandeur or a feeling that the world is against him.

8. A person who reports hearing strange voices or shows evidence of being disoriented to time, place, or person, perhaps even assuming statue-like poses for extended periods or refusing to talk.

9. The pronounced alcoholic, the person with uncontrolled homosexual tendencies, or the person who continually lies or steals without purpose.

10. An extremely depressed person who seems to have lost any meaning in life and perhaps threatens suicide.

11. One who persists in a kind of happiness that does not ring true, probably covering a deep-rooted problem.

These are only a few of the symptoms evidenced by extremely disturbed people. The list could be many times longer. But the point is this: A Christian lay counselor's beginning of wisdom is a keen understanding of his own limitations of training and experience for the counseling situation. Most people are normal, and there are enough of them with problems to keep the Christian lay counselor busy without involving himself in psychological disturbances beyond his depth.

Counselors must approach their task with gentleness and humility. The depth of the human mind, the scope of personality, the sacredness of life, and the precious meaning of an immortal soul are ideas which cannot be dealt with casually or carelessly. The Christian counselor will use the best skills he can command, but knows full well that much of the good done in counseling will have to be done in spite of his own frailties and mistakes. God must work with him in helping people if his counseling task is to be effective. Like the Christian surgeon who depends upon his skills in the operating room, plus the help of the Great Physician, the counselor depends upon counseling skills plus the whole counsel of God which works through human personality, through God's written Word, and through prayer. The prayer of the Christian counselor is not only for the person he will help, but for himself.

CHAPTER 17

How God Works
Through Counseling

An important and significant question asked by many is this: How does God work in the counseling process? He does so (1) through human nature, (2) through His Word, (3) through prayer and meditation, and (4) through the enlightened understanding of the counselor.

Does God speak directly to men? The Bible record indicates that He has!

South of the Syrian city of Damascus at high noon on a midsummer day, God spoke to a Jew who carried the official credentials of the Sanhedrin. The voice said: "I am Jesus whom thou persecutest. But rise, and stand upon thy feet: for I have appeared unto thee for this purpose, to make thee a minister and a witness both of these things which thou hast seen, and of those things in the which I will appear unto thee."

Thirty years later Paul stood before the throne of King Agrippa in Caesarea to be judged. After recounting his vision on the Damascus road, Paul said, "Whereupon, O king Agrippa, I was not disobedient unto the heavenly vision." For the full length of his ministry, Paul was sustained, comforted, and guided by the voice of God which had spoken directly to him at the time of his conversion.

The Bible record also includes similar experiences of the "counsel of God" in the lives of others, including such men as Moses, Elijah, Peter, and John the Beloved, plus many lesser known Bible characters.

Even in modern times, God seems to impress some persons with clear-cut counsel they never seem tempted to doubt. For instance, ministers and missionaries do not enter the ministry as a vocation, but as a calling. Most of them can tell of definite experiences in which they received their call. David Livingstone, George Müller, Harmon Schmelzenbach, Phil Saint, to name only a few, have received definite impressions from God which were real enough to dominate their decisions and direct the course of their lives.

But instead of solving problems by the direct intervention of His voice, God more often helps counselors and the people who seek their help to use their own enlightened judgment. When Solomon became king, he sought the Lord for counsel, saying, "Give therefore thy servant an understanding heart . . . that I may discern." The Bible takes account of the fact that this prayer pleased the Lord.

And today it seems to please the Lord to give people insight into their own problems. In fact, many clinically trained Christian counselors believe that God has provided intelligent human beings with the capacity to find a way out of their mental and spiritual hang-ups. In most cases only a minimum of guidance is needed, if any at all.

In a very mysterious and wonderful way, God seems to work through human nature. We often hear such phrases as:

"Then all of a sudden the light dawned."

"From then on, I saw things differently."

"The pressure was gone; the resentment was taken away."

"I don't know what happened, but at once I began to see myself as I really was."

"I seemed to have a judgment and understanding that was beyond myself."

"It was wonderful; all at once I seemed to see and understand my problem—for the first time."

"I realized that the situation had not changed, but I had. From then God began to give me new strength, even physical strength, for the load I carried."

If God has provided human beings with the capacity to gain insight and understanding into their own problems, why is it so difficult for people to gain this understanding? The answer to this question is very complicated and involves considerably more discussion than is allowed for here. Here are a few suggestions:

1. People are subjective instead of objective. This means they tend to see every problem from their own personal point of view instead of the perspective of a third disinterested party.

2. People have prejudices. A prejudice is a special kind of feeling, a disposition or prejudgment, people have toward certain things, situations, or people. Prejudices are increased by interpreting all new information in the light of the already existing feelings. Prejudice may be either in favor of or against—positive or negative.

3. People have fear of failure, or of looking bad to someone else. Lest he look bad in the eyes of someone from whom he craves acceptance and approval, a person will tend to ignore his own problems, to misrepresent them to himself, or simply to keep quiet about the difficulties which bother him.

4. People have limited judgment and experience. Youth is not the only reason for limited human understanding. Lack of learning, narrow life style, and emotional immaturity all contribute to limited judgment and experience.

In order to overcome these and other such limitations which people have, the counseling situation must provide: (1) an opportunity for the person to talk out his problems with a mature, understanding person in whom he has confidence, and (2) a non-threatening atmosphere in which he fears neither discipline nor being thought less of for the problems which he presents. Under these conditions, God seems to release within persons this capacity to understand their own problems.

One of the big problems of the beginning counselor is to have patience—to really believe that God will help people to understand their problems, and to give Him time to do so. The temptation is to try to hasten the process by "telling him" what he should do, or what the basic difficulty is. The process of letting enlightened judgment work is slower and requires considerable more patience on the part of the counselor, but it is by far the most effective way, and also the most rewarding aspect of the counselor-counselee relationship.

The importance of the Bible in counseling cannot be overemphasized. In fact, people expect their counselors in the church to know and use God's Word. Many things have changed since the Bible was first written, but it is still a relevant Book. Human nature is much the same as it has always been. The first humans to fly into outer space were not much different in basic nature from the fishermen of Galilee who became the first disciples of Jesus. It is therefore part of the counselor's opportunity and duty to help people see that the Bible has meaning for their problems today.

The writer to the Hebrews knew the power of the Word when he said, "For the word of God is quick, and powerful, and sharper than any twoedged sword, piercing even to the dividing asunder of soul and spirit, and of the joints and marrow, and is a discerner of the thoughts and intents of the heart."

Paul also knew the value of the Bible to human nature and spiritual problems when he wrote in his second letter to Timothy, "All scripture is given by inspiration of God, and is profitable for doctrine, for reproof, for correction, for instruction in righteousness."

The Bible poorly used in the counseling situation may, however, be a detriment if not a downright danger.

1. A mechanical use of the Bible is to be deplored. To tell a frustrated person to "go read the Bible" may only provoke him and close the door to any further opportunity for spiritual help. A glib recitation of memory verses to a woman filled with anxiety may only indicate to her that the counselor has no comprehension of her problem. Favorite verses of scripture which have proved to be a source of personal help to one may, to others overcome with problems, be meaningless and even add to a growing state of confusion. God indeed speaks through His Word in a most miraculous and wonderful way, but not in a mechanical application of the Bible to human problems.

2. There is danger in applying the Bible without explanation. An ancient prophet said, "They know not the thoughts of the Lord, neither understand they his counsel." Although most Christian counselors are familiar with principles of good Bible interpretation, many people can scarcely think of the Bible except in literal terms.

A teen-ager, considerably upset, once came to my office with this problem. Someone, upon hearing his story of some problems with his classmates, told him simply to go and read the Sermon on the Mount and put it into practice. The boy followed this advice but found that it only further complicated his own problems. His original trouble in school had come because another boy had stolen his jacket. But in the Sermon on the Mount he read that, if anyone took away "thy coat, let him have thy cloak also." Furthermore, Jesus said, "Whosoever shall compel thee to go a mile, go with him twain. Give to him that asketh thee, and from him that would borrow of thee turn thou not away."

3. Another dangerous use of the Scriptures is to emphasize the negative aspects of the Word. Sensitive persons, for instance, have developed neurotic fears over the sin against the Holy Ghost. This happens when this truth has been emphasized to the exclusion of the love of God. Some are inclined to refer to the Ten Commandments more than to the Beatitudes, to Good Friday more than to Easter morning, to the Cross more than to the empty tomb. "Thou shalt not" takes precedence over such biblical words as love . . . forgiveness . . . joy . . . comfort. Repentance can become an end in itself without the emphasis upon forgiveness. Commandments can become more dominant than the enabling promises.

The Bible is God's Word and must be taken as a whole, both negative and positive. It restricts, but only to enable. It reproves, but only to bless; chastises, but only to improve. The Bible is not a burden, but a blessing; not a blinding headlight, but a guiding Lamp for the pathway. Therefore all applications of the Bible to the specific problems brought to the counselor must be applied in such a manner as to help relieve the problem rather than add to or confuse it.

God not only speaks through human nature and through His Word, *but* He also communicates with men and women by the means of prayer and meditation. Jesus said, "If two of you shall agree on earth as touching any thing they shall ask, it shall be done for them of my Father which is in heaven." This verse seems to be particularly appropriate to the counseling situation since the promise is to two persons who shall agree on a given problem.

However, great difficulty can center around the use of prayer in the counseling process. The person who has never practiced prayer and is suddenly thrust into a spirit of fervent prayer concerning his own personal problems may even get a wrong idea of the purpose of praying. His ideas on prayer will be further confused if nothing happens to relieve his problem. It may appear that God is either unable or unwilling to answer either his own prayer or that of the counselor.

People with problems often gain little satisfaction from their prayers. They carry the same tensions into their prayer life that exist in their other activities and they call upon God for help in a frame of mind that defies His help. In such cases, the counselor's task is to make prayer more meaningful for them.

It is fitting for the Christian counselor to conclude his counseling conversation by offering a brief, sincere prayer to God. The very spirit and manner manifested by him during this prayer can become an inspiration. It should be offered in the same conversational tones which were used during the the counseling conversation. Some persons tend to assume a kind of strange voice when they enter into prayer. Be natural.

The prayer should deal directly with the problem at hand, not by reciting the issues to God, who already knows, but by speaking frankly about the problem, accepting it as it exists, and asking divine help in a solution. Here, in substance, is the prayer I prayed after a session with a young man who was frustrated over a broken engagement.

> Our Father in heaven, we thank Thee for the opportunity thou hast given to George and me to discuss his problem together. We have tried to think through the various issues which disturb him but realize that our own understanding is limited and that we have difficulty in expressing in words the feelings that we have within ourselves. As George goes today, we pray that Thy Spirit will continue to direct his mind, that Thou wilt help him to overcome the frustrations he so keenly feels, and that this problem shall resolve itself into better understanding and more Christian maturity for George. These things we humbly and sincerely pray, knowing that Thou art a Heavenly Father who desires to help us in the problems we face. In the name of Christ, our Savior, we pray. Amen.

Not only is prayer meaningful in the counseling room, but often individuals need to be taught how to pray privately. People who desire to learn better how to pray must be taught the importance of quietness and meditation. An effective prayer life does not develop in the midst of a hurried schedule. A few moments each day at a regular period are much more meaningful in developing a prayer life than long periods of desperate prayer during times of great frustration and anxiety.

Furthermore, prayer is a two-way communication. This means that individuals must learn to listen for the voice of God as well as speak to Him. At least half the time in prayer may be spent profitably in silence. God can speak only to those who will listen.

And further, a meaningful prayer life involves naturalness. It is contradictory to believe that God is with us and then to pray to Him like He lived on the far side of the most distant planet. With a natural flow of communication whereby the person expresses himself to God and in silence waits for the voice of God to speak to him, prayer can be lifted out of the realm of the mysterious up onto the plain of practical daily living.

The Christian counselor prays for judgment, for patience, and for serenity. All of these important characteristics may be improved with experience and practice, but he must still rely heavily on the leadership of the Spirit. God seems to supply the right statement, the right question, or the right approach to a specific problem at just the time when it is needed most. This enlightened judgment, so much needed, God will grant to the sincere counselor, and will increase it day by day.

Patience, too, is a capacity which can be enlarged. The counselor needs the patience of the farmer who sows the seed, cultivates, waits for the harvest, and does not despair even if the harvest fails. He must have a patience which does not allow him to lose faith in humanity, a patience which endures in spite of discouragement.

And the prayer of the counselor is for serenity in spite of pressures. To get upset, to become impatient or harsh, to make quick value judgments, and to jump to conclusions are ruinous in the counseling situation. But God gives calmness to those who seek it.

CHAPTER 18

Counseling Teen-agers

There is no single set of counseling techniques which may be called correct while all others are incorrect. Counseling is helping people through purposeful conversation on the problems which have become disturbing. Each teen-ager comes with a unique problem peculiar to himself. In each instance, then, the counselor responds in the way which is most appropriate. Sometimes the good Christian counselor does nothing more than provide himself as a sounding board for the gripes and complaints of persons who need "to tell somebody." When things are off his chest he feels better and, without expecting any change in his circumstances, he is ready to take up life again. Part of the counselor's job is to absorb a certain amount of explosive guff which young people need to expend after a tension buildup.

On occasion, the counselee is hesitant to talk about his problem and the counselor needs to draw out the story with leading questions, such as, "If there is some more of the problem that you would like to tell me, I would be glad to hear it." Or sometimes the counselor needs only to say, "That is interesting; tell me more." Sometimes silence on the part of the counselor will make the teen-ager feel compelled to re-phrase the problem or explain it more fully.

Then again, it may be a talkative teen who will go on and on about his problem, taking the initiative in exploring all angles of the situation. In this case, the counselor needs only to summarize or concentrate on the feelings being expressed. This is done by such remarks as, "You feel very keenly about this, don't you?" or, "I can see this problem has a long his-tory."

But regardless of the specific technique which the coun-selor uses in a given situation, one basic consideration must always be kept in mind: *Counseling takes time*. The volun-teer Christian counselor is often plagued by lack of time. But if he enters into a counseling relationship with a teen-ager, he should plan to see the problem through. Unless he can give time to it, more harm than good may be done.

Each individual has a complex personality. Problems are often interrelated, and they almost always have a his-tory. Also, the person often has been building up tension—even over the decision of coming to talk with the counselor in the first place. Therefore the teen who is frustrated over interrelated problems which have been building up over a period of time generally needs several unhurried conversa-tions with the pastor, teacher, or whomever he has gone to for help. The more intense and upset the person is, the more time is needed. The longer the problems have been building up, the longer the time needed to resolve them. Further, this principle of taking time to solve problems implies that the process of assisting individuals is a continuous one. It will take several sessions.

A generation ago William Rainey Harper, then the president of the University of Chicago, made a famous speech in which he pointed out the importance and significance of differences among teen-agers. He said concerning a student's course of study:

> There should be a diagnosis of each student, in order to discover his capacity, his taste, his tendencies, his weaknesses, and his defects; and upon the basis of such a diagnosis his course of study should be arranged. Today the professor's energy is practically exhausted in his study of the subject he is to present to the student. In the time that is coming, provision must be made either by the regular instructor or by those appointed especially for the purpose, to study in detail the man or woman to whom instructions are offered.

If the study of individual differences among teen-agers is important in the high school or college teaching-learning situation, it is all the more important to the Christian counselor in the church.

First, it is important to notice that teen-agers differ greatly in physical characteristics such as height, weight, and general attractiveness. By the age of 15 a teen-ager may be six inches taller and 20 pounds heavier than other boys of his age. At the age of 17 the slower growing boys may catch up with the first. Meanwhile, the differences between them in physical development are usually accompanied by other differences, particularly in the degree of interest in girls, leisure-time activities in which they are interested, and personality development. These latter differences require different modes of adjustment. The slower developing teen may feel inadequate and even develop feelings of inferiority. At the same time the rapidly developing boy may feel very self-conscious and may already be entering into a conflict with his family as to whether he is to be treated as a child or as an adult.

In a small-church group of junior high students, in a certain church, all of the youngsters were considered average except Ruth and George. Ruth, a 13-year-old, was an early maturing girl and already quite a young lady. Her appearance and interests were not those of the other girls in the group. George was a late maturing boy. He was short with a childlike face and would rather play with younger boys than associate with the 13-year-olds in his group. Both George and Ruth were social misfits for a time. They found excuses to avoid the parties and other social gatherings of their group. They attended Sunday school because they were forced to by their parents, but sat quietly, almost sullenly, refusing to speak or otherwise participate in any way that might draw attention to themselves. At home they found fault with the church, were critical of the other youth group members, and seemed to be losing interest in religion. They were further frustrated by the alarmed parents who kept reminding their confused 13-year-olds, "I don't understand you; we've brought you up to love the church and now you are so different. Is the church any different now than before?"

Both Ruth and George, who came from unrelated homes, had a common problem. They were not maturing at the same rate as the other children. By direction from a wise counselor, they were helped through a period in life that might otherwise have been much more painful and could even have become the breeding ground for chronic emotional problems. These problems which grow out of differences in physical traits are so commonplace that they are likely to be disregarded.

Besides physical differences, teen-agers also differ in their mental abilities. Some are more intelligent than others; they catch on more quickly, grasp new ideas, and are quicker to see the point at issue. There is also a difference in their specific aptitudes, such as the ability to speak or sing, to make things with their hands, or to deal with abstract ideas. Further, teen-agers differ in emotional characteristics. Some are more optimistic than others. Some are easily irritated; others are placid. Some teens make social contacts easily and enjoy a sense of social well-being, while others struggle painfully when talking to new people.

Next to these perhaps the most easily recognized are the emotional differences. Consider, for example, the variations in emotional responses of teen-agers to a frustrating situation such as this: A girl is waiting to meet a boy but he fails to appear. In this situation one girl is amused, another annoyed, another downright angry, and a fourth worried. Furthermore, in the same situation the girls react in different ways on different days, depending on such factors as their physical well-being and general emotional tone.

Problems have a history. A child psychologist was once asked, "When does the training of a baby begin?" His cryptic answer was, "One hundred years before he is born." Even before the child comes into the world, forces are at work which will make their impact upon the baby's teen years. The intelligence and physical characteristics of a teen-ager's parents, the economic status of the home, whether or not the baby was wanted, and even the way his parents have learned to handle their own problems—all of these are factors at work before the child is born that will influence him for good or ill during later years.

All childhood experiences, particularly those heavy with emotional content, make their contributions to the adult outlook. The kind of church life, school experiences, and especially the way the child learns to handle his problems will contribute to making him the kind of person he eventually becomes. All of the things that have ever happened to him become a part of his personality. The things he enjoys most, the things he dislikes, his sense of values, and most important, his ideas of himself, are all a product of this background.

Not all teen-agers are walking problems. Most are normal, and most of the problems they have are those common to their contemporaries. When a young person is emotionally high one day and then borders on despondency the following, he is not necessarily mentally ill. He may be suffering from the periods of moodiness which are characteristic of teen-agers whose bodies are growing rapidly, whose newly acquired sensitivity to the opposite sex causes inner confusion, and whose social skills are inadequate for the demands of society.

A typical youth problem is the battle to break away from the domination of adults, particularly those of his family, and striving to be accepted by them as an equal. This sometimes causes strange kinds of behavior. Bursts of anger, even against his parents, and streaks of extreme independence are all evidence of the battle he is waging for equal rights as an adult.

The point is this: Very few young people are mentally ill. Most of the problems which they face are those involved in facing life and are just part of growing up. This does not mean they need no help. They need counselors to whom they may go with their problems, who understand them, and who will cooperate with them in working out solutions.

A young lady from a strict church background was frustrated concerning a decision whether or not to marry a Catholic boy. The problem spilled over into several areas of her life. Her grades dropped in school. She lost the leadership of her youth group at the church, which formerly had been unquestioned, and in the home she engaged in a violent running battle with her parents. This serves to illustrate that problems do not occur singly. A problem in one area of life will almost always create problems in other areas.

Furthermore, most problems have more than one cause. Back to the case of the young lady: Several factors intensified the problem in her proposed marriage to the Catholic boy. Most acute and emotional was the religion issue, of course, but there were others. The girl had joined with her parents in planning a college career which would be eliminated by the marriage. She had suffered quietly from the fear of going through life unmarried. And more, the young lady had gone through her life carrying out the decisions made by her parents. She suffered from an intense desire to make decisions on her own.

Therefore, the counselor must beware of isolating single problems and relating them to single causes. Both problems and their causes come in clusters.

How a teen-ager feels about his problem is often more important than the facts in the case. One reason for this is the general feeling of inadequacy he has in trying to express in words his feelings about his problems. And the more deeply personal the problem is, the more difficult it is for him to speak adequately about it. Such words as "home" and "love" may have immensely different meanings to the counselor and the teen-ager. And if they come from extremely different backgrounds, they will have all the more difficulty in communicating.

Another reason why feelings are often more important than the facts of a case is that emotions are difficult to express in speech. Young people many times do not like to tell adults about their emotional experiences. What one says, moreover, makes an impression on the counselor quite different from what he intended to convey.

A father once brought his 15-year-old son to my office as a result of a dispute over discipline in the home. After accusations and denials, the laying down of the law and a rejection of the law, the two of them had finally agreed to ask the pastor to arbitrate the dispute. The immediate issue concerned late hours at a drive-in. For over half of the one-hour interview, we got nowhere, because I thought they were speaking of a drive-in restaurant, and the boy and his father were talking about a drive-in movie. Until this point was clarified in my thinking, what was being said was somewhat confusing to me. It can be, then, that the counselor and the teen-ager may be thinking in two different worlds of ideas.

Dr. Carl Rogers at the University of Chicago teaches that each individual lives in his own little world of experience. He reacts to things as he sees them at the moment, whether or not he sees them correctly. For instance, two men driving at night on a road in Idaho may see an object loom up in the middle of the highway ahead. The passenger who has lived all of his life in the East sees the large object on the highway as a big bolder, and reacts with real fright. He presses the floorboard as if slamming on imaginary brakes, and braces himself for the expected impact. He yells for the driver to stop. But the other man, a native of the country, pays no heed. He sees the large object in the highway as a familiar tumbleweed and reacts with nonchalance. Each of the men reacts to the object in the highway as he sees it. The fright experienced by the easterner is just as real as though the tumbleweed had been made of granite.

If a teen-ager has strong emotions about a particular subject, even though he sees it in a wrong light, the counselor must concentrate on these emotional feelings and endeavor to understand them. Only then can he give guidance that may change those emotions. Better still, his goal should be to help the teen-ager to move from an emphasis on "feeling" to a concentration on "thinking" about his problem.

Every teen-ager has a mental picture of himself. And he behaves according to his own idea of what he is like. If he sees himself as a debonair "young man about town," he will behave accordingly. Or if he sees himself as a rejected and misunderstood person, he will behave in accordance with this mental idea he has of himself. This is why Dr. Rogers writes, "The best vantage point for understanding behavior is from the internal frame of reference of the individual himself." The teen-ager who sees himself as a brilliant student will excuse himself for a failure in one subject because it does not fit his picture of himself. Or the girl who pictures herself as the prettiest teen-ager in the class will find ways of explaining the choice of another girl as campus queen.

When a teen-ager does behave in a manner which is out

of character with this picture of himself, he often rejects responsibility for his action. He simply says, "It just wasn't me; I don't behave like that. I am not that kind of person." Or again he may say, "I really was not responsible for what I was doing." One of the problems which the teen-ager faces in maturing is to create a mental picture of himself which is in harmony with facts as they are. To this end, a good Christian counselor may often be of help.

If a young person sees himself as a spiritual leader, he is often confronted with what to do with his attitudes and ways of behavior which are not consistent with this mental picture. If he endeavors to continue handling his problem by denying or rejecting the idea that such attitudes and behavior exist, or if he tries to rationalize his way around every episode which is not consistent with this picture, very severe spiritual and emotional tension can arise.

Therefore the counselor must ask those questions which will help to clarify the mental picture the teen-ager has of himself.

Since all behavior points to underlying personal needs and satisfactions, it is important that counselors know what these needs are. Whenever a person shows signs of inner tensions or whenever his behavior suddenly shifts patterns, the counselor knows that there has been a change in his underlying needs. Some of these needs are as follows:

Food, water, fresh air, sunshine, adequate clothing, and shelter are basic physical needs. Even in this day of food surpluses, malnutrition remains a problem with many young people. This does not mean necessarily that the teen-ager is not fed enough; it means that he may not be getting the right food. And then it must be remembered that teen-agers burn up huge amounts of energy. Young people seem to thrive on a schedule that is far too fast and long for their elders. The whirl of social activities, part-time jobs, schoolwork, family life, and even church activities, can often tax the physical capacities even of the young. While they are having fun and enjoying new experiences, teen-agers can build up considerable tensions over physical needs. The youth leader needs to watch his group for danger signals.

Even when the physical needs of the teen-ager seem to be adequately cared for, a young person still may not function properly from a physical point of view. The girl who seems to learn slowly may need only corrective glasses. Or the boy who tends to daydream may suffer from impaired hearing. The seemingly lazy teen-ager may be anemic even though he looks healthy enough. Or the emotionally high-strung teen-ager may have a glandular problem. The counselor needs to be alert to the special kinds of teen-age problems which need the attention of a medical doctor.

Human nature being what it is, teen-agers also have certain social and emotional desires which need to be fulfilled.

1. Teen-agers need friends. Some persons conceive hell as a life of total aloneness. One of the worst prison punishments is solitary confinement. A life without contacts with other human beings is simply biological existence. Teen-agers need to talk with each other, to share experiences, to probe the unknown and the mysterious, to give and receive fellowship. The teen-ager who does not find a satisfying fulfillment of this need will suffer from problems which grow in intensity as he grows older.

2. Teen-agers need personal recognition. Every human being yearns to be recognized. "It is better to be hated than ignored." In this world of automation and push-button machines, Erich Fromm deplores the fact that men are becoming like machines, and machines are becoming more like men. Big cities and large high schools are factors which tend to minimize the importance of the individual. A teen-ager's registration number at the university, his social security num-

ber, or his driver's license may become more important than his name. But no person wants to be merely a number. Each wants to be a person who is needed and wanted—one who belongs. The counselor working with teen-agers in the church should help to fulfill this need.

3. Teen-agers need status. Every collection of persons is consciously or unconsciously organized into status groups according to their worth to others. Teen-agers have their system of status rating. Each strives to gain status by approval from other teen-agers and from adults. He likes to think that he is doing something worthwhile and likes to see evidences of his climbing up the status ladder.

4. Young people need to learn how to live with authority. Man must live with authority from the cradle to the grave. Teen-agers must learn to deal realistically with authority figures at various levels. Those who have lacked love or have suffered harshness at the hands of adults during the years of their childhood will tend to react negatively to those who exercise authority over them or those who symbolize authority. Some, for instance, who have resented the kind of authority they have experienced at the hands of their mothers in the home will also reject the authority of a female teacher in school. But regardless of its cause, teen-agers who are going to live happily in this complex, highly organized society must learn to live with authority in all of its various forms.

5. Teen-agers need a personal commitment. Through participation in various group activities at school and in the church, the teen-ager becomes committed in some degree to the common goals toward which most of his friends are working. By the time he is ready to graduate from high school, he is asking and answering for himself questions about his own purposes in life. He is beginning to decide what things are most important. Much of his behavior can be understood by observing the things which he believes

matter most, those which matter little, and those which do not matter at all. A philosophy of life is beginning to be crystallized. His attitude toward religion which is taking form will likely endure. The teen-ager feels a need to find those things which are big and lasting, to which he may give himself in commitment. This will be true in several phases of his life, including religion, vocation, and academic preparation.

Teen-age conduct may often appear to be utterly senseless from an adult point of view. But when the youth acts in what seems to be a highly inappropriate manner, it is best for the counselor to look behind the behavior itself to determine what need the teen-ager may be trying to fulfill. The unskilled youth leader may try protest, preaching, punishment, or good advice, but none of these tactics will be very effective in changing teen-age behavior. Only as the basic needs of youth are understood and met can there be hope for fundamental changes in the direction of an improved adjustment.

In the process of assisting the teen-ager, help should be given in such a way that he gains his own understanding and makes his own decisions. This means that a counselor does not tell the teen-ager immediately and directly what he thinks the teen-ager's problems are or what he believes the solution to any of these problems is. Rather, it means that the counselor assumes an attitude that encourages the teen-ager to develop his own insight, to make his own decisions, and to act upon his own best judgment. The counselor may provide helpful information, he can assist in exploration and analysis, and can even make suggestions, but the final decisions and plans must be those of the teen-ager. No other procedure is effective.

THE
PARALYSIS
OF ANALYSIS

CHAPTER 19

A Self-study for a Local Church

Government bureaus and educational institutions are notorious for the multiplication of self-studies. A need arises. Obvious options are offered as solutions. But about that time some person fearful of failure calls for a study; and what has been called "the paralysis of analysis" begins. By the time the study is made, the nature of the problem is changed. The solutions don't fit. So makeshift measures are imposed while additional studies and analyses are undertaken.

The same dynamics obtain with persons trying to cope with personal emotional problems. With magazine articles, hearsay, and a selective book list, troubled persons start to analyze themselves. And a creeping emotional paralysis begins. The more they try to analyze themselves, the more fearful they become. Emotions shift. Strange new symptoms develop. And short-circuited by limited knowledge, the emotional paralysis continues to creep.

In Chapter 3 the minus-plus pastor was described as a person who felt everyone else had the answers needed to meet his church's needs. Fearful of himself and his own proneness to failure, the minus-plus pastor finds it easy to forestall action decisions by instituting one more study by an "expert."

Most pastors would do well to dig a hole in the ground and bury their fear of failure, deep down. God's good air should be breathed in deep. All self-doubt should be exhaled and announcement with faith and enthusiasm made concerning plans for church growth. Then work should begin with an enthusiasm and vigor which indicates there is no doubt the dream will become fulfilled.

Too much time has been spent in self-study if the effort results in the paralysis of analysis. But having said all these negative things about analysis, it still is a good thing to "know thyself." A self-study does have value, if it is determined in advance that the analysis will result in decisions of positive action.

Many self-studies for churches become self-defeating because of rigid categories in square footages, funds, and "people statistics." Success or failure in the ministry is a relative thing. How far the church has come or gone is more important than where it is. A church of considerable membership which has been losing its effectiveness over a period of years is sick, even if it remains larger than most other churches. Likewise, a church with a small membership may be healthy if it is moving in the right direction toward increasing effectiveness. It is the extent to which things are happening and trends developing that really matters.

The following self-study tool is devised to help evaluate the extent to which a church is moving or to find out if it has become static. It is intended only as a tool to help describe accurately the status of a given church. The men who devised the concepts on which the tool is built believe these are the crucial points which make the difference between movement and non-movement, between effectiveness and non-effectiveness in a given church.

There are no standards as such. The results of this study are completely subjective. They are worth whatever they are worth to you. There are no right or wrong answers, only honest responses.

With this background of warning, guidelines, and limitations, use this self-study to the best advantage in understanding your church and your ministry. After filling in the blanks and studying the profile of your church and your ministry, go back to study carefully the concepts of growth and effectiveness which have been built into this tool.

The first step in the analysis of a given church is to determine if it is (1) dying, (2) just sustaining itself, or (3) growing.

THE DYING CHURCH

1. *A church is dying to the extent that the membership and attendance continue to fall over a period of years.*

   1A. Indicate your *church membership* for each of the last five years:
   - (1) _____
   - (2) _____
   - (3) _____
   - (4) _____
   - (5) _____

   1B. Indicate your *Sunday school average attendance* over the same five-year period:
   - (1) _____
   - (2) _____
   - (3) _____
   - (4) _____
   - (5) _____

   1C. What is the *numerical increase or decrease* in your church membership over the past five years?

   _____

   1D. What is your *numerical increase or decrease* in average annual Sunday school attendance over the past five years?

   _____

1E. What is the *percentage of increase or decrease* in church membership over the past five years?

_____

1F. What is the *percentage of increase or decrease* in annual average Sunday school attendance over the past five years?

_____

2. *A church is dying to the extent it is less able to support its financial needs.*

2A. What is the *total raised* for all purposes during each of the past five years?

(1) _____
(2) _____
(3) _____
(4) _____
(5) _____

2B. What has been the *pastor's salary* and cash benefits for each of the past five years?

(1) _____
(2) _____
(3) _____
(4) _____
(5) _____

2C. How much has the church given to *world missions, home missions, district budget, and educational budget* in each of the past five years?

	World Missions	Home Missions	District Budget	Educational Budget
(1)	_____	_____	_____	_____
(2)	_____	_____	_____	_____
(3)	_____	_____	_____	_____
(4)	_____	_____	_____	_____
(5)	_____	_____	_____	_____

2D. Is the total amount given for these benevolences during each of the past five years equal to at least 20 percent of the total money raised for all purposes?

_____ Yes _____ No

3. *A church is dying to the extent it is not able to supply its own lay leadership.*

3A. To what degrees is the *leadership* in the administration and teaching staff of the *Sunday school adequate?*

_____ Superior
_____ More than adequate
_____ Adequate
_____ Less than adequate
_____ Very poor

3B. To what extent is the *church board adequate* to cope with the problems of the church?

_____ Superior
_____ More than adequate
_____ Adequate
_____ Less than adequate
_____ Very poor

3C. To what extent is the *music staff adequate?*

_____ Superior
_____ More than adequate
_____ Adequate
_____ Less than adequate
_____ Very poor

3D. To what extent is the leadership of the *NYPS adequate?*

_____ Superior
_____ More than adequate
_____ Adequate
_____ Less than adequate
_____ Very poor

3E. To what extent is the *NWMS leadership adequate?*

____ Superior

____ More than adequate

____ Adequate

____ Less than adequate

____ Very poor

4. *A church is dying to the extent that members moving out of the area are not being replaced.*

4A. How many people have left the church in the past 18 months?

_____

4B. How many people have started coming to the church in the past 18 months?

_____

5. *A church is dying to the extent that the church facilities become less and less equal to the level of the expectations of the congregation and the community.*

5A. How would most of your congregation feel about the *cleanliness* of your church building?

____ Superior

____ More than adequate

____ Adequate

____ Less than adequate

____ Very poor

5B. How would most of the people in your congregation feel about the level of *maintenance* of your church property?

____ Superior

____ More than adequate

____ Adequate

____ Less than adequate

____ Very poor

5C. How long has it been since your church was *redecorated?*

_____

THE SUSTAINING CHURCH

The first step above a dying church is a church which is just keeping itself "even with the board." It is just doing the things that keep it alive by replacing losses with equal gains, but is experiencing little or no growth. The characteristics of the sustaining church are as follows:

1. *A church is sustaining itself to the extent it is able to hold its own statistically in membership, in total money raised for all purposes, and in Sunday school average attendance.*

    1A. What is your five-year record of *membership?*

        (1) _____
        (2) _____
        (3) _____
        (4) _____
        (5) _____

    1B. What is your record of *money raised* for all purposes?

        (1) _____
        (2) _____
        (3) _____
        (4) _____
        (5) _____

    1C. What is your five-year record of average *Sunday school* attendance?

        (1) _____
        (2) _____
        (3) _____
        (4) _____
        (5) _____

2. *A church is sustaining itself to the extent all budgets are met.*

    2A. What is your *educational budget* record for the past five years?

        (1) _____
        (2) _____

(3) _____
(4) _____
(5) _____

2B. What is your *district budget* record for the past five years?

(1) _____
(2) _____
(3) _____
(4) _____
(5) _____

2C. What is your *world missions* giving record for the past five years?

(1) _____
(2) _____
(3) _____
(4) _____
(5) _____

2D. What is your *home missions budget* record for the past five years?

(1) _____
(2) _____
(3) _____
(4) _____
(5) _____

3. *A church is sustaining itself to the extent it is able to meet all its own local budget needs, including a full-time minister.*

3A. Does your church board feel it is paying a *salary adequate for full-time* service?

Yes _____   No _____

3B. How does the *salary compare* to a beginning schoolteacher with an A.B. degree in your community?

Above _____   Same _____   Below _____

3C. To what degree is the church able this year to

pay *its obligations* on *debt* services, current *operating* costs, and *benevolent* giving?

> Mortgage payments _____
> Current operating
> costs _____
> Benevolent giving _____

4. *A church is sustaining itself to the extent the children of the church are being taught basic Bible knowledge.*

4A. Test *three sixth-graders* who are members of church families and have attended the church for at least four years. Although the test below is selective, how well can they do in supplying the following answers?

> _____ Books of the Old Testament
> _____ Books of the New Testament
> _____ First psalm
> _____ Twenty-third psalm
> _____ Beatitudes
> _____ I Corinthians 13
> _____ Ten Commandments
> _____ Names of four apostles
> _____ Place where Jesus was born
> _____ Where in the Bible is the Sermon on the Mount found?
> _____ Where did Moses live?
> _____ Who was Abraham's son?
> _____ Who was the father of Joseph?
> _____ Name three parables of Christ.
> _____ Name three miracles of Christ.

4B. What percentage of the *primary and junior workers* in your church can supply answers to the above test?

_____

THE GROWING CHURCH

If a church has reversed its losses and has begun to do those things that will make it self-supporting, the next step up is to become a growing church. The growing church is moving away from the status quo toward an effective ministry. The characteristics of the growing church are as follows:

1. *A church is growing to the extent the statistics continue to increase over a period of years.*

   1A. Over a five-year period, what have the church membership statistics been *each* year?
   (1) _____ Increase _____
   (2) _____ Increase _____
   (3) _____ Increase _____
   (4) _____ Increase _____
   (5) _____ Increase _____

   1B. Over a five-year period, what have the average Sunday school attendance statistics been *each* year?
   (1) _____ Increase _____
   (2) _____ Increase _____
   (3) _____ Increase _____
   (4) _____ Increase _____
   (5) _____ Increase _____

   1C. Over a five-year period, what have been the total monies raised for all purposes *each* year?
   (1) _____ Increase _____
   (2) _____ Increase _____
   (3) _____ Increase _____
   (4) _____ Increase _____
   (5) _____ Increase _____

2. *A church is growing to the extent the increases in church membership and average Sunday school attendance indicate the church is developing its evangelistic outreach in relation to its population potential.*

   2A. Determine from the local Chamber of Commerce or from a census tract available in the public library the *rate of growth* in:

    ____ (a) your region
    ____ (b) your state
    ____ (c) your city
    ____ (d) your neighborhood

2B. How do the increases or decreases in population statistics compare with your local statistics in Sunday school attendance and church membership? Is your church keeping up with the population increase?

Below ____ Equal ____ Above ____

3. *A church is growing to the extent the increase in membership and attendance reflects a balanced family range of age-groups.*

3A. Compare your local age-group *statistics* (percentage of total enrollment) with the typical evangelical Sunday school as follows:

Yours National
____ 3% crib and one-year-olds
____ 5% two- and three-year-olds
____ 8% Kindergarten
____ 14% Primary
____ 14% Junior
____ 9% Junior high
____ 8% Senior high
____ 4% Single young adults (18-24)
____ 35% Adults (married and/or above 24)

4. *The church is growing to the extent that the total raised for all purposes meets the needs of the increasing congregation.*

4A. Has giving tended to keep pace with numerical growth? Yes ____ No ____

4B. Does the number of tithers or systematic givers increase as the attendance has increased? Yes ____ No ____

4C. Is the income sufficient to expand the program of the church to meet the needs of the increased numbers? Yes _____ No _____

CHAPTER 20

The Ideal Church
and Pastor

The ideal church does not exist. Neither does the ideal pastor or the ideal anything. Perfection in human terms is something to strive for, not something to achieve.

But if there are degrees of perfection or dimensions of the ideal, then the ideal church with the ideal pastor is a dream to pursue. And as long as we work to make a dream come true, we guard ourselves against the possibility of a nightmare of frustration.

As guidelines for discussion in group meetings, here are the characteristics of an ideal church and ideal pastor from one man's point of view.

THE IDEAL CHURCH

1. *The ideal church functions comfortably within the framework of the denomination in matters of doctrine and policy.*

Doctrine at its best is man's explanation of God's grace.

By their nature, doctrinal statements have strengths and weaknesses and are always selective rather than exhaustive or all-inclusive. A good debater or clever lawyer generally can build a case against the most carefully worded statements, if disposed to do so.

Theological dogma is not supposed to be a set of exhaustive, finalized statements on a given theme of God's grace. Even the best minds of good, committed men who agree generally on doctrinal points of view will often differ vigorously over some points. Because of man's limitations, no absolutely perfect doctrinal statement has been devised. But the effective church functions comfortably within the doctrinal framework of the denomination without burning up much needed spiritual energies fighting real or imagined heresy in each other.

In matters of church government, the situation is the same; there is no perfect system of church organization. But the ideal church does not spend its energies negatively on weaknesses in the system, but views the denominational structure and the hierarchy of the church as resources for helping the local church do its job better. The denomination is not a monster to strangle the local church but an enormous reservoir of strength, guidance, and resources to help the local church accomplish its purpose. The ideal church understands this and functions joyfully within the system.

2. *The ideal church is characterized by a spirit of optimism, enthusiasm, and anticipation concerning its pastor, its members, its program, and its services.*

In the ideal church, everybody anticipates every Sunday with great enthusiasm. Sunday is an event, not a day. Enthusiasm is not worked up or put on. It is just there because the church is meeting people's needs in many ways. Because the church is meeting their needs, the congregation loves the pastor, the personnel, and the programs. The services are inspiring. The Sunday night service brings back the whole family. And the auxiliaries, such as Sunday school, teen program, music, and children's activities, are geared for every member of the family.

3. *The ideal church views finances as a means to an end, not an end in itself.*

Lots of money is raised in the ideal church but without struggle and pressure. The people have a clear concept of the programs the money pays for. Money is not raised for survival, but for personnel and programs which meet needs. The church is not easily sidetracked into a building program that makes bricks and mortgages more important than people.

4. *The ideal church uses every imaginative method possible to serve people and bring persons to know the risen Christ as Lord and Master of their lives.*

According to some records, the altar was first used in New York City about the time Andrew Jackson became president of the United States. A mourners' bench or altar for seekers was not used by the Apostle Paul, Martin Luther, or John Wesley. However, the altar is a very important piece of church furniture and should be used often and to good evangelistic purpose.

But the ideal church coordinates with its use of the altar other kinds of evangelism. Personal witnessing, small groups, fellowship evangelism, pastor's class, and many more methods may be used to bring people face-to-face with Christ. The ideal church is conservative in its theology and liberal in its methods of outreach.

5. *The ideal church has a deep commitment to growth and expansion which results naturally in increased statistics.*

Laymen are not motivated to Christian service by berating sermons which are used like cudgels to browbeat them. But laymen will take hold of handles their size. They respond to assignments which fit them. The effectiveness of church programs depends considerably on success factors built into advance planning. When a large pattern is cut which includes reasonable assignments for numbers of people, the natural result is more people. And people working in the Kingdom at jobs they enjoy are happy people attracting other people to the same Lord and the same local church.

6. *The ideal church has adequate physical facilities to care for an expanding pattern of growth which involves increasing numbers of laymen at work.*

There is no substitute for laymen. They are what it is all about in the church. The church is happy, radiant, redeemed people working together in helping, healing, and loving the people of the world as well as each other.

THE IDEAL PASTOR

1. *The ideal pastor is an authentic human being with self-respect, feelings of adequacy in Christ which help him relate well to other human beings in his own home, in his church, and in the world outside.*

Unless the pastor is an authentic, genuine human being, nothing else matters. The stained-glass voice cannot cover up the broken windows of a man's soul. No Sunday performance is ever enough to offset continuing poor notices on the other six days. No black clerical cloth can ever be tailored to cover a tarnished reputation—at least not for long. The makings of a good preacher begin with a good man.

2. *The ideal pastor has developed his skills in communicating the gospel of Jesus Christ as good news.*

People do not need to go to church to be told what they ought to be or what they are not. Most of them knew full well their failures before they left home. But everyone needs help in knowing how to do what he already knows he should be doing. This is the good news of the gospel. The ideal pastor does not scold and whip. He illuminates the gospel of Christ to the needs of the people. He demonstrates with logic and illustration how the gospel is applied to people's needs. This is good news. He preaches this word with enthusiasm and joy just because it *is* good news.

3. *The ideal pastor believes in longer pastorates and sees himself as being in the very place God wants him to be.*

Few things are more satisfying to the pastor and the congregation than a deep sense of God's hand on the pastoral leadership of the local church. The long look makes it possible for God to use a man in the fulfilling of His purposes in a community. Short pastorates make for unstable congregations.

4. *The ideal pastor is disciplined in time management, study habits, and personal finance.*

Few people have a more open opportunity for the abuse of time than does a pastor. He has to be his own self-starter and stopper. He carries his own punch clock and stopwatch, and he signs his own time card. Habits of time management are closely related to the other personal disciplines of study habits and personal finance. These, too, must be mastered by the ideal man of God.

5. *The ideal pastor is able to live happily in the denominational framework and still feel freedom of personal expression and professional fulfillment.*

Men who leave the denomination rarely do so for theological reasons; they leave because of their inability to function happily within the denominational framework. Theology is just the rationale. The only person who can criticize the church constructively is the man who loves the church and is committed to it. No one is expected to accept any organizational structure blindly. But whether it be in industry, in an educational institution, or in a denomination, the effective man has come to terms and lives at peace within the organizational structure.

6. *The ideal pastor is dominated by the twin virtues of love and purity.*

It was love and purity that turned the world upside down in the time of the apostles. In a culture of violence, perversion, and materialism, the one power the Romans could not stop was the power of a humble Christian life dominated by love and purity.

Reference Notes

Chapter 7:
   1. William Barclay, *In the Hands of God* (New York: Harper and Row, 1966).
   2. *Ibid.*
   3. Gerald Kennedy, *For Laymen and Other Martyrs* (New York: Harper and Row, 1969).
   4. *Ibid.*

Chapter 16:
   1. Edward S. Bordin, *The Psychology of Counseling* (New York: Appleton-Century-Crofts, 1968).

Suggested Reading

Anderson, Camilla M. *Saints, Sinners and Psychiatry.* Portland, Ore.: The Durham Press, 1950.

Barclay, William. *In the Hands of God.* New York: Harper & Row, 1966.

Barnette, J. N. *The Pull of the People.* Nashville: Convention Press, 1956.

Bayly, Joseph. *The Gospel Blimp.* Havertown, Pa.: Windward Press, 1960.

Berne, Eric. *A Layman's Guide to Psychiatry and Psychoanalysis.* New York: Simon and Schuster, 1968.

Bristol, Claude M. *The Magic of Believing.* Englewood Cliffs, N.J.: Prentice-Hall, Inc., 1964.

Clinebell, Howard J., Jr. *Basic Types of Pastoral Counseling.* Nashville: Abingdon Press, 1966.

———. *Mental Health Through Christian Community.* Nashville: Abingdon Press, 1965.

Edwards, Gene. *How to Have a Soul Winning Church.* Springfield, Mo.: Gospel Publishing House, 1962.

Frankl, Viktor E. *Man's Search for Meaning.* New York: Washington Square Press, Inc., 1963.

Howe, Reuel L. *The Miracle of Dialogue.* New York: The Seabury Press, 1966.

Hulme, William E. *Your Pastor's Problems: A Guide for Ministers and Laymen.* Garden City, New York: Doubleday & Company, Inc., 1966.

Kennedy, Gerald. *The Seven Worlds of the Minister.* New York: Harper and Row, 1968.

Lush, Ron. *Use Them or Lose Them.* Kansas City: Nazarene Publishing House, 1968.

Maltz, Maxwell. *Psycho-Cybernetics*. Hollywood, Calif.: Wilshire Book Company, 1965.

May, Rollo. *The Art of Counseling*. Nashville: The Abingdon Press, 1939.

McGavran, Donald Anderson. *How Churches Grow*. London, W. 1: World Dominion Press, 1963.

Moberg, David O. *The Church as a Social Institution*. Englewood Cliffs, N.J.: Prentice-Hall, Inc., 1962.

Niebuhr, H. Richard. *The Social Sources of Denominationalism*. Hamden, Conn.: The Shoe String Press, 1954.

Oliver, Robert T. *The Psychology of Persuasive Speech*. New York: Longmans, Green and Co., Inc., 1957.

Parrott, Leslie. *Easy to Live With*. Kansas City: Beacon Hill Press of Kansas City, 1970.

———. *The Usher's Manual*. Grand Rapids, Mich.: Zondervan Publishing House, 1970.

Parrott, Lora Lee. *How to Be a Preacher's Wife and Like It*. Grand Rapids, Mich.: Zondervan Publishing House, 1969.

Purkiser, W. T. *The New Testament Image of the Ministry*. Kansas City: Beacon Hill Press of Kansas City, 1969.

Raines, Robert A. *New Life in the Church*. New York: Harper and Row, 1961.

Sanders, J. Oswald. *Spiritual Leadership*. Chicago: Moody Press, 1967.

Schuller, Robert H. *Move Ahead with Possibility Thinking*. Garden City, N.Y.: Doubleday & Company, Inc., 1967.

Shanafelt, Ira L. *The Evangelical Home Bible Class*. Kansas City: Beacon Hill Press of Kansas City, 1970.

Smith, Charles Merrill. *How to Become a Bishop Without Being Religious*. Garden City, N.Y.: Doubleday & Co., Inc., 1965.

Trueblood, Elton. *The Incendiary Fellowship*. New York: Harper and Row, 1967.

Turnbull, Ralph G. *A Minister's Obstacles*. Westwood, N.J.: Fleming H. Revell Company, 1964.

What, Then, Is Man? A Symposium of Theology, Psychology, and Psychiatry. St. Louis: Concordia Publishing House, 1958.

Williamson, G. B. *Overseers of the Flock*. Kansas City: Beacon Hill Press, 1952.